IMAGES OF WAR

WAFFEN-SS ON THE WESTERN FRONT

RARE PHOTOGRAPHS FROM WARTIME ARCHIVES

Ian Baxter

Pen & Sword
MILITARY

First published in Great Britain in 2013 and reprinted in 2021 by
PEN & SWORD MILITARY
An imprint of
Pen & Sword Books Ltd
47 Church Street
Barnsley
South Yorkshire
S70 2AS

ISBN 978-1-78159-185-7

Typeset by Concept, Huddersfield, West Yorkshire HD4 5JL.
Printed and bound in England by CPI Group (UK) Ltd, Croydon CR0 4YY.

Pen & Sword Books Ltd incorporates the imprints of Pen & Sword Archaeology, Atlas, Aviation, Battleground, Discovery, Family History, History, Maritime, Military, Naval, Politics, Railways, Select, Social History, Transport, True Crime, and Claymore Press, Frontline Books, Leo Cooper, Praetorian Press, Remember When, Seaforth Publishing and Wharncliffe.

For a complete list of Pen & Sword titles please contact
PEN & SWORD BOOKS LIMITED
47 Church Street, Barnsley, South Yorkshire, S70 2AS, England
E-mail: enquiries@pen-and-sword.co.uk
Website: www.pen-and-sword.co.uk

Contents

Introduction

This book in the popular *Images of War* series covers the deeds of the Waffen-SS from its inception in the 1930s to war in the Low Countries, France, the Balkans, Yugoslavia, Greece, Italy and finally on the Western Front in 1944; and to the defence of the bombed and blasted ruins of the Reich during the last weeks and months of the war in 1945. This is a comprehensive illustrated study of the Waffen-SS in action and features action photographs of such famous divisions as the *Leibstandarte Adolf Hitler*, *Das Reich*, *Totenkopf* and a number of rare shots of the *Polizei* Division in action in all theatres of operations.

About the Author

Ian Baxter is a military historian who specializes in German twentieth-century military history. He has written more than forty books including *'Wolf': Hitler's Wartime Headquarters*, *Poland – The Eighteen-Day Victory March*, *Panzers In North Africa*, *The Ardennes Offensive*, *The Western Campaign*, *The 12th SS.Panzer-Division Hitlerjugend*, *The Waffen-SS on the Western Front*, *The Waffen-SS on the Eastern Front*, *The Red Army At Stalingrad*, *Elite German Forces of World War II*, *Armoured Warfare*, *German Tanks of War*, *Blitzkrieg*, *Panzer-Divisions At War*, *Hitler's Panzers*, *Panzer Markings of World War Two*, *German Armoured Vehicles of World War Two*, *German Guns of the Third Reich* and most recently *The Last Two Years of the Waffen-SS At War*, *SS of Treblinka*, *Höss – creator of Auschwitz*, *Auschwitz Death Camp*, *Battle of the Baltics*, *Battle for the Reich*, *Last Years of the German Army* and *Concentration Camp Guards*. He has also written over 100 articles including 'Last Days of Hitler', 'Wolf's Lair', 'Story of the V1 and V2 Rocket Programme', 'Secret Aircraft of World War Two', 'Rommel At Tobruk', 'Hitler's War with his Generals', 'Secret British Plans to Assassinate Hitler', 'SS At Arnhem', 'Hitlerjugend', 'Battle Of Caen 1944', 'Gebirgsjäger at War', 'Panzer Crews', 'Hitlerjugend Guerrillas', 'Last Battles in the East', 'Battle of Berlin', 'Destruction of Busse's Ninth Army' and many more. He has reviewed numerous military studies for publication and supplied thousands of photographs and important documents to various publishers and film production companies worldwide.

Chapter One

Training for War

Between 1933 and 1939 the power of the SS grew considerably with thousands of men being recruited into the new ideological elite armed formation under the command of Heinrich Himmler. All early recruits were expected to meet very stringent criteria. Every volunteer had to be fit, have excellent racial criteria and produce a certificate of good behaviour from the police. During their tough training programme new recruits were indoctrinated with an almost fanatical determination to fight for the Führer, even if it meant risking life and limb on the battlefield. Each recruit then left, displaying blind allegiance and joined one of the newly-created armed SS divisions where he would obey every order, even if it meant shooting prisoners and committing atrocities against civilians.

The initial training was carried out in various depots outside each *SS Verfügungstruppe* (SS Replacement Troop) regiment's home town. The training programme was very tough and demanding. Out on the rifle ranges the recruits became used to their weapons, and once familiar they were taught infantry assault techniques that included charging at sandbags with fixed bayonets. Every instructor placed great emphasis on aggression on the battlefield, with an ardent determination to win at all costs. It was believed that this kind of training enhanced every recruit and instilled in them the drive to overcome their enemy through fighting skill and sustained physical endurance. Every candidate was pushed to the limits of tolerance. They were constantly sent on long marches with or without their kit, in order to develop stamina and endurance.

At least three times a week the trainees had to endure formal lectures covering policies of the Nazi Party, which included a very in-depth indoctrination in SS philosophy. The men were all ordered to follow Heinrich Himmler's demand for blind and absolute obedience and learnt to treat those who were against the Reich with fanatical hatred. This included Jews, gypsies, homosexuals, the political Left and any other groups deemed to be inferior beings. By perpetually drilling the recruits to hate, they were able to infuse them with pitiless contempt and to not think twice about meting out severe punishments. The training in Nazi ideology was relentless. Not only did they learn about enemies of the state but were also indoctrinated into SS philosophy regarding racial superiority. These ideological teachings were aimed at producing men who ardently believed in the new Aryan Order. Regularly they had to attend lectures ful of anti-Semitism. On the bulletin boards inside the SS barracks and canteen there were often copies of the racist newspaper *Der Stürmer*. Such propaganda material was routinely circulated in order to ferment hatred and violence. As a result many of the new recruits became easily susceptible to anti-Semitic doctrine, especially the younger men.

In this manner, the SS was filled with men fully indoctrinated into fighting for their Führer, regardless of their own fate. With anti-Semitism ingrained in their minds, every candidate would be willing to obey any order, even those involving the killing of prisoners and atrocities against civilians. Such was the strength of feeling manufactured against those who did not conform to the Aryan ideal.

At an SS training barracks in 1939. These troops are from the newly-created regiment known as *Germania*. In October 1939 the *Deutschland*, *Germania* and *Der Führer* regiments were organized into the SS-*Verfügungs* Division. These would soon form part of the infamous *Das Reich* Division.

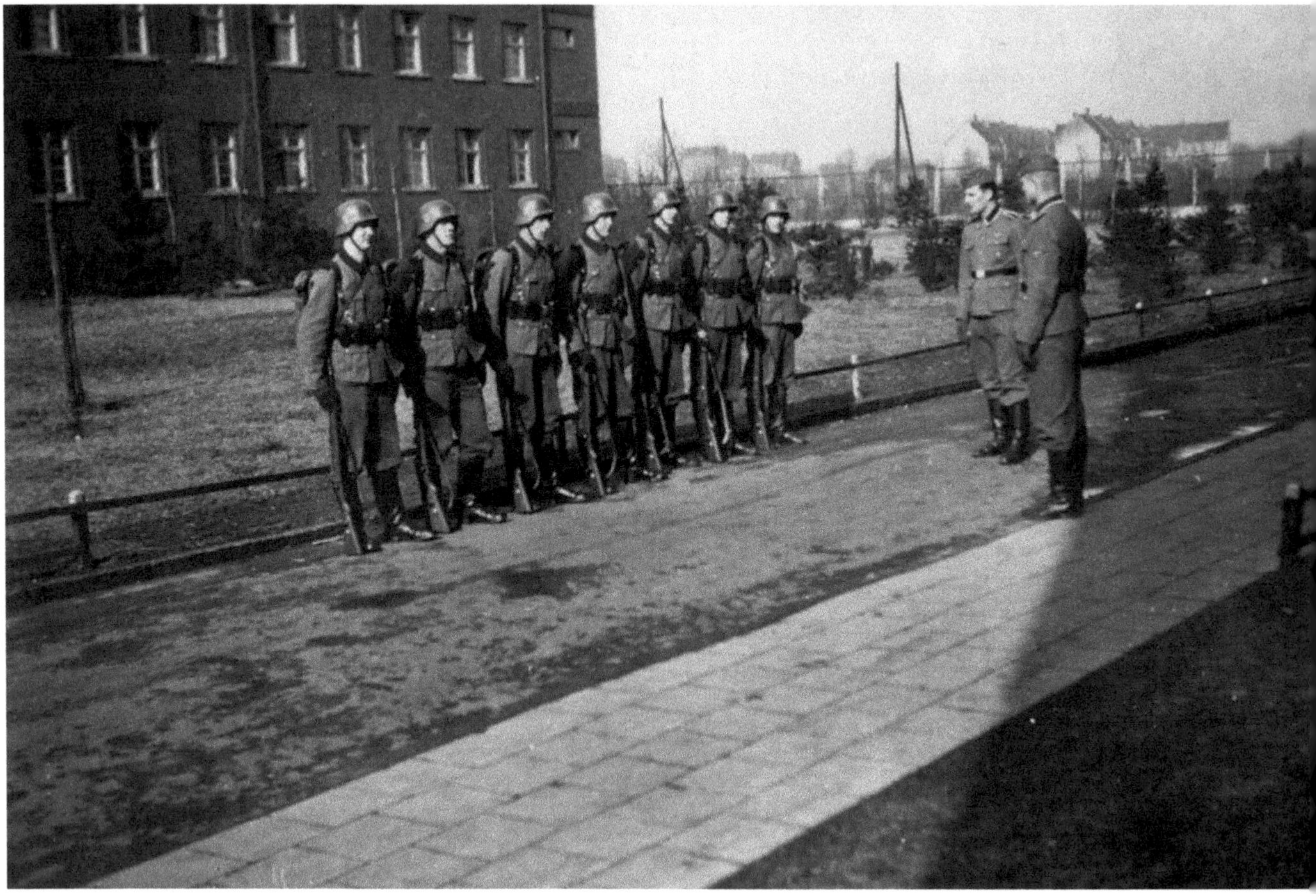

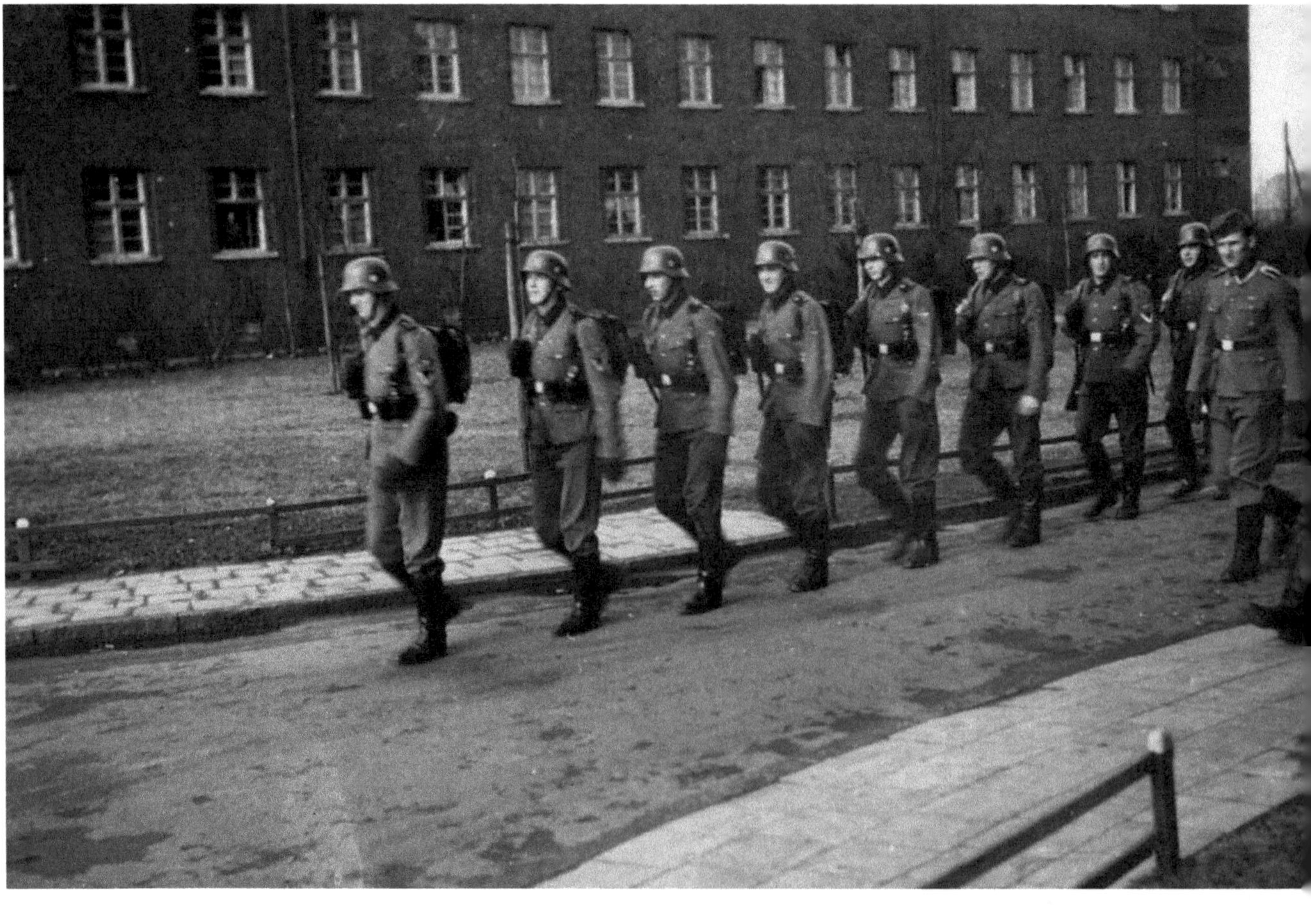

Three photographs at an unidentified barracks: these SS troops are training, during which every trainee was pushed to the very limits of his endurance. These men were constantly sent on long foot marches with or without full kit, in order to develop stamina and endurance.

A group photograph of the SS at a training barracks with their commanding officers. In the early stages of SS recruitment every new volunteer had to conform to excellent racial features and produce a certificate of good behaviour from the police. Although the recruitment programme for the volunteers was very selective, the training was equally tough.

Two photographs showing an SS military procession: one shows them playing while at their home station in Germany; in the other the troops can be seen in a town. As a walking-out dress this uniform proved to be impressive when on parade but was not practical for field use or other utility purposes. Note the grey-white cotton drill uniform being worn by the soldiers at the barracks. This was produced in the summer of 1933 for training purposes for the *Heer* and later the Waffen-SS as well.

A photograph taken in the winter of 1939 showing the commanding officer inspecting the men of the SS *Totenkopf* (Death's Head) Division. This division was formed in October 1939, initially from concentration camp guards of the 1st (*Oberbayern*), 2nd (*Brandenburg*) and 3rd (*Thüringen*) *Standarten* regiments of the SS-*Totenkopfverbände* and soldiers from the SS-*Heimwehr Danzig*. The division was commanded by the fanatical SS-*Obergruppenführer* Theodor Eicke and prior to it achieving division status, the formation was known as *Kampfgruppe* (battle group) Eicke.

A photograph showing an SS *Totenkopf* barracks. The period of enlistment in the original *Totenkopf* was initially four years. However, by 1938 this had trebled to twelve years. Before joining, all recruits served as conscripts in the armed services. Although this was intended to give them basic military training, not all recruits were very happy undergoing another spell of military service once they had completed their national service. It was not until May 1939 that Hitler finally directed that serving in the *Totenkopf* would count as compulsory military service.

A motorcyclist with his motorcycle combination. Initially motorcyclists were often part of a reconnaissance battalion that comprised a battalion staff, motorcycle company and heavy company. However, as the war continued many of the motorcyclists were used for dispatch purposes to various sections of the front and because motorcycles were regarded as versatile machines it enabled them to move swiftly across terrain with important information. The marking on the sidecar denotes a Commissariat unit – in this specific case, that of a motorized bakery unit.

Members of the *Totenkopf* during training with their commanding officer. The officer wears the standard army greatcoat and field cap with the infamous death's head badge that soon symbolized the *Totenkopf* Division on the battlefield of both Western and Eastern Fronts.

A *Totenkopf* commanding officer checks the magazine of one of his trainees as he is put through firing practice in the snow. The weapon is the ancestor of the British BREN gun, the ex-Czechoslovakian Army ZB vz 26 or 30 light machine gun, which all fell into German hands with the annexation of Bohemia-Moravia. The ZB vz 26 and ZB vz 30 were both very expensive to produce but gave good service; they are extremely difficult to differentiate externally.

A group of *Totenkopf* troops at a concentration camp. Most of these soldiers were initially taken from the concentration camp system and then recruited into the Waffen-SS for military service. By the time these men fought on the battlefield most were already physiologically hardened and imbued with fanatical hatred, both against political opponents of the Reich and those regarded as racially impure. These men were ideal candidates to wreak often terrible crimes both on and off the battlefield.

A *Totenkopf* machine-gun crew in the snow during a training exercise. Once these men were familiar with their weapons they were taught infantry assault techniques that included charging positions with live ammunition. The SS were taught that 'the only form of defence on the battlefield is to attack'. Such aggressive training led to inevitable fatalities but the SS were firm believers in the 'train hard, fight easy' school of thought. The training also made the average SS man much more inclined to lay down his life for the Führer.

The following sequence of photographs shows a full military ceremony in honour of a *Totenkopf* soldier who had been fatally injured. The national flag has been draped over the coffin and the soldier's M1935 steel helmet displaying the SS insignia on the side has been placed in traditional style on top of the coffin as a mark of respect.

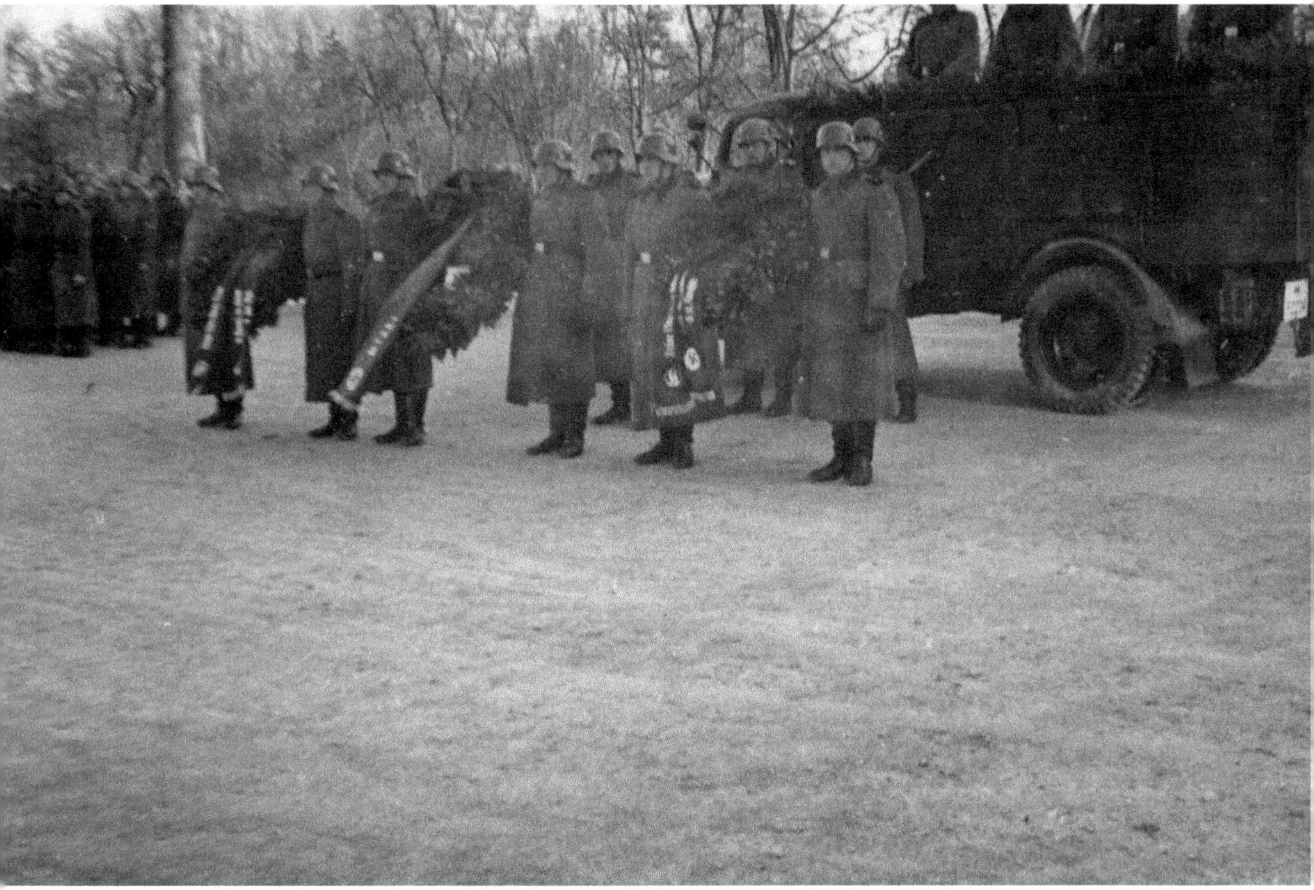

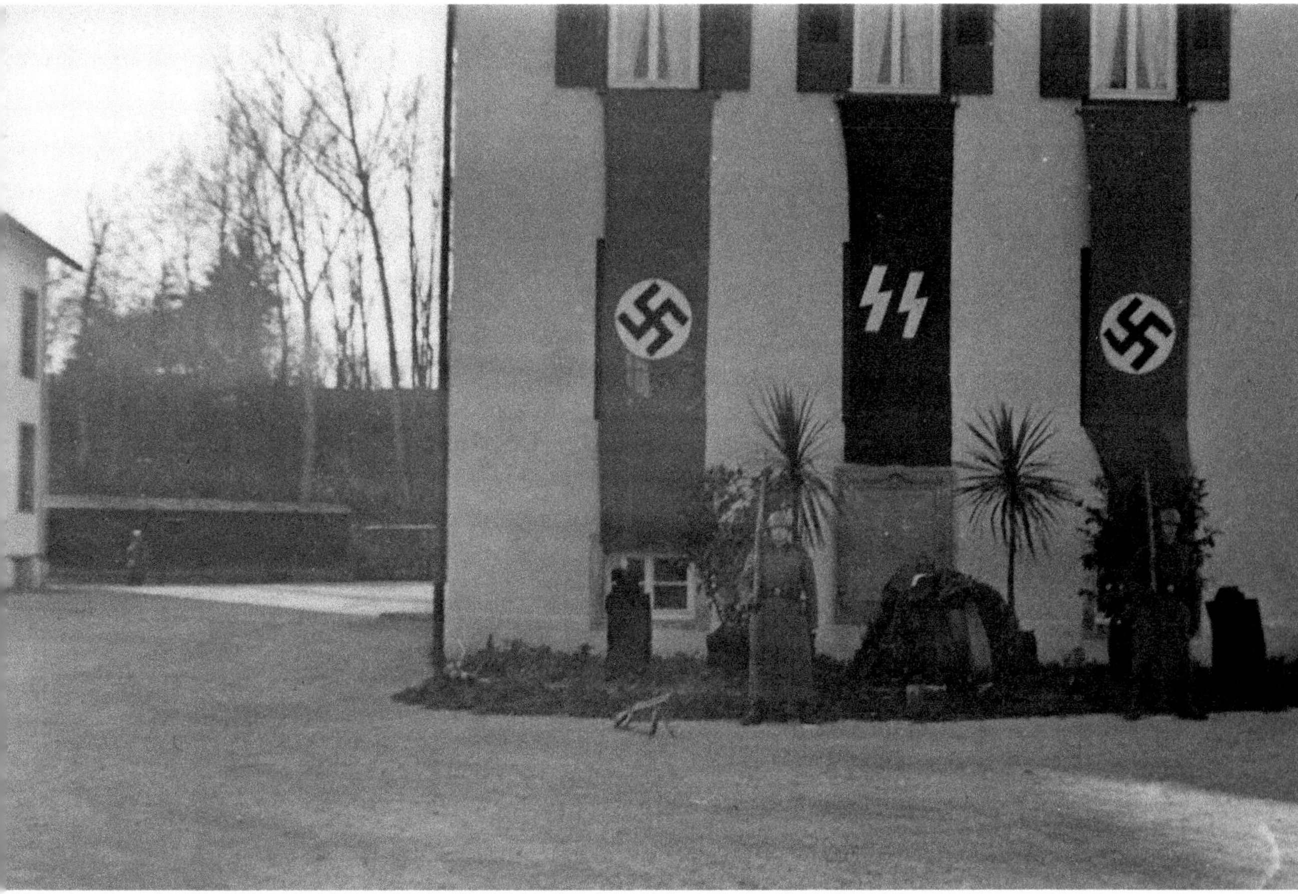

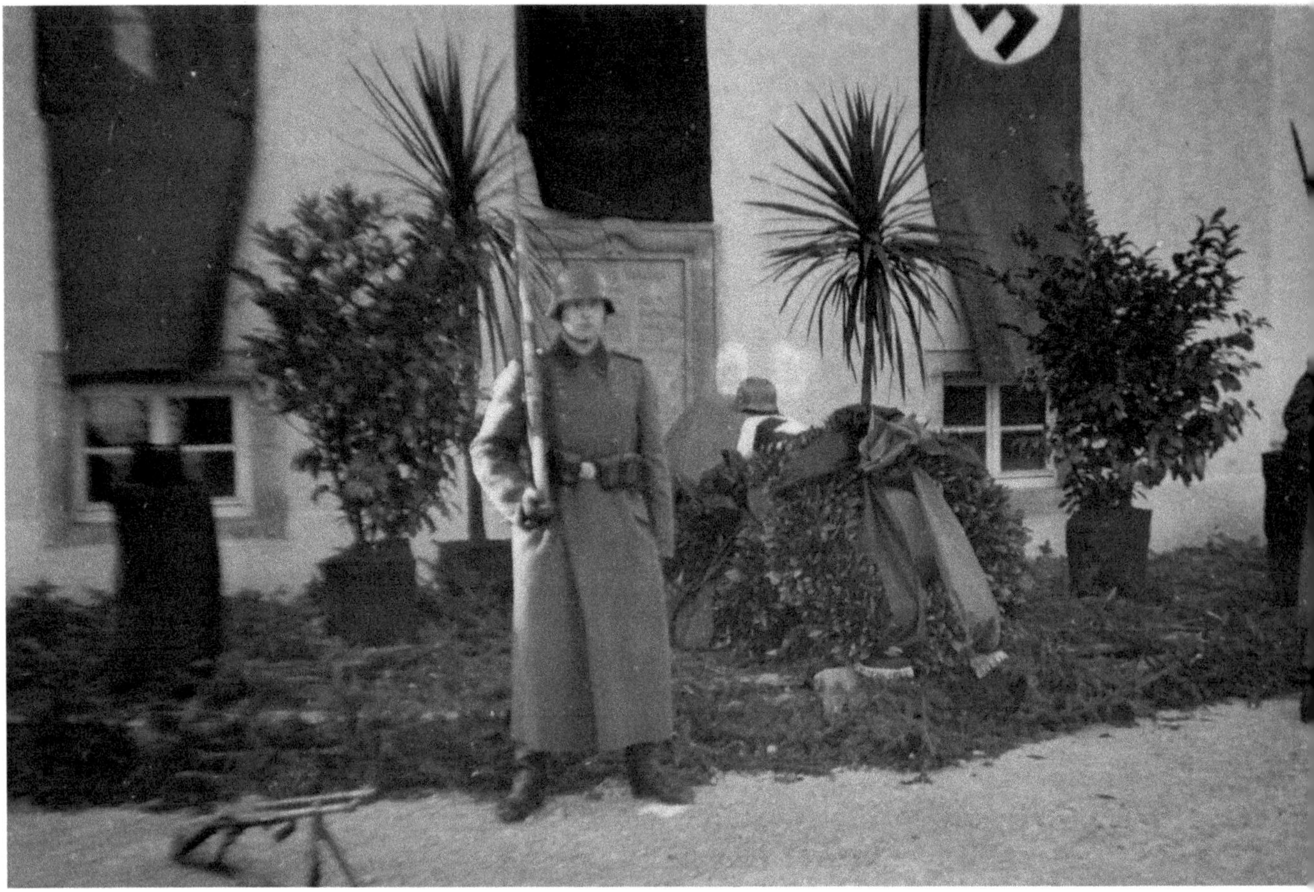

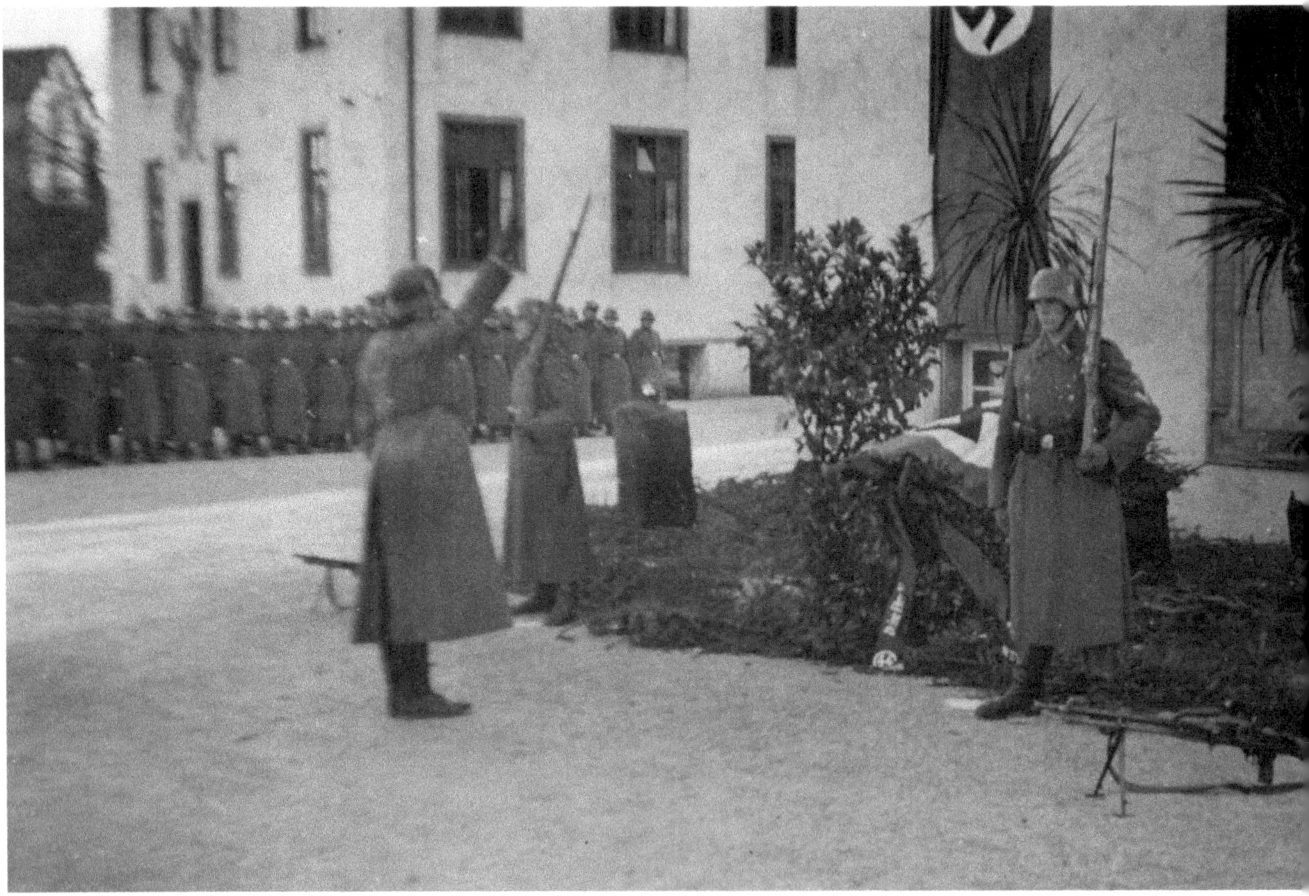

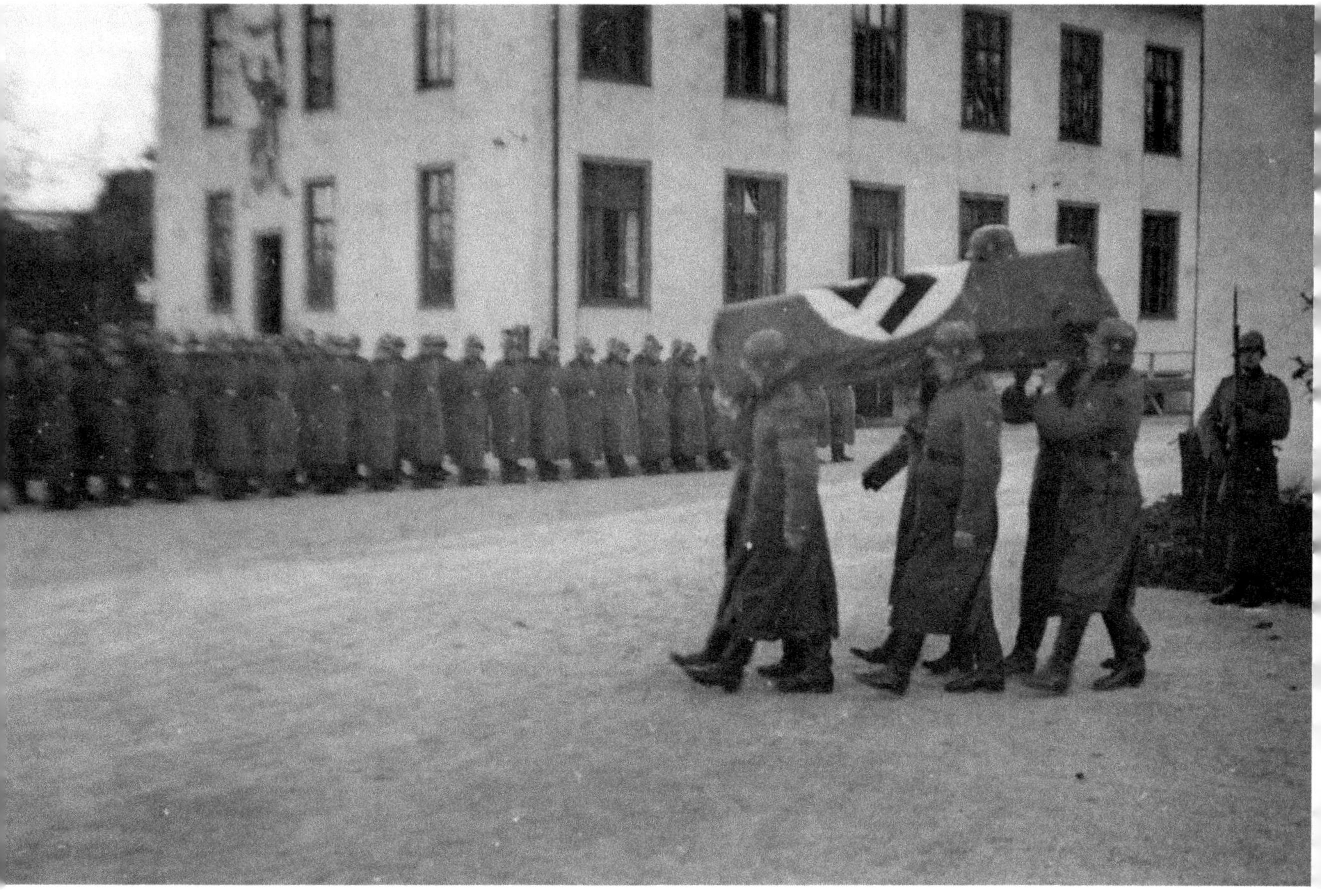

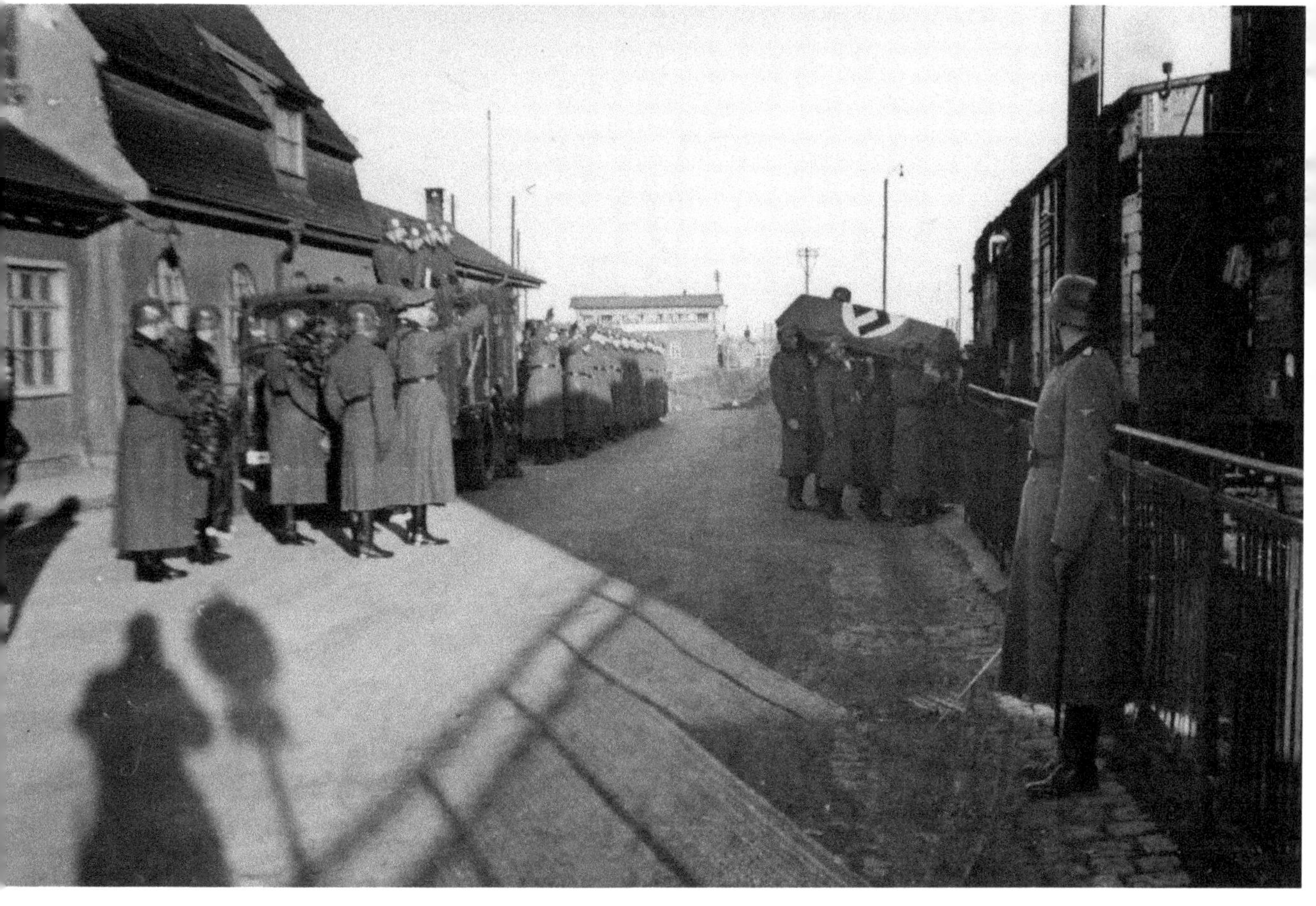

An honour guard of the *Totenkopf* follows the field banner standard during a march from their barracks. To many of the SS men the field banner had an almost religious significance. Each banner was 'consecrated' by Hitler himself at the *Reichsparteitage* (Reich party convention days) in Nuremberg where it was brought into contact with the *Blutfahne* (Blood Banner), the flag stained with the blood of Nazi 'martyrs' killed during the Munich Putsch of 1923.

At a training barracks these SS men in their striped cotton drill training clothes are seen with a light Horch cross-country vehicle. Note the number plate on the rear with the SS insignia emblazoned above the five-digit number.

During a training exercise, two *Totenkopf* troops: one armed with the standard 98K carbine bolt-action rifle and the other with the new machine pistol (MP38). These men in training regarded their role in the SS as unlike that of their *Heer* counterparts. Their blind faith in Adolf Hitler enabled them to go into combat with fanatical allegiance to the Führer and with the ability to face the prospect of almost certain.

Totenkopf troops on a march from their barracks with their commanding officer leading them on horseback. The training of these men was designed to create a perfect political fighting machine and proved a great attraction to the men who joined. They ardently believed that stretching themselves both physically and mentally marked them as true Nordic Germans, complete and proven men of Hitler's military elite.

A *Totenkopf* unit on the march through a German town from a training barracks. Young children, some of whom are dressed in the *Hitlerjugend* uniform, watch this military spectacle. All of the *Totenkopf* troops are dressed in the inadequately insulated *Heer* greatcoat which would be standard issue until the end of 1941 when these men nearly froze to death in the depths of a Russian winter.

A portrait photograph of a young SS soldier, probably from the *Leibstandarte* SS. He wears the M1935 steel helmet with the SS insignia on the right-hand side. The SS rune is sewn onto his tunic.

A military band of the *Leibstandarte* can be seen playing during a training procession at a barracks.

Totenkopf troops practising with the MG34 machine gun in a heavy role. The MG34 would soon prove an invaluable weapon to the SS, both in a defensive and offensive role. This machine gun would be used extensively throughout the war and would become a much feared and revered weapon.

This and the following two photographs show troops of the *Totenkopf* marching during the winter. Their commanding officers can be seen accompanying the march. Commanders strove at length to teach their men that they were part of a closed order with its own rules and regulations. The men soon understood the meaning of obedience, honesty and dedication to duty. From the very first day they were recruited into the SS and put into training, they were told that they were part of a military elite totally separate from their *Heer* counterparts.

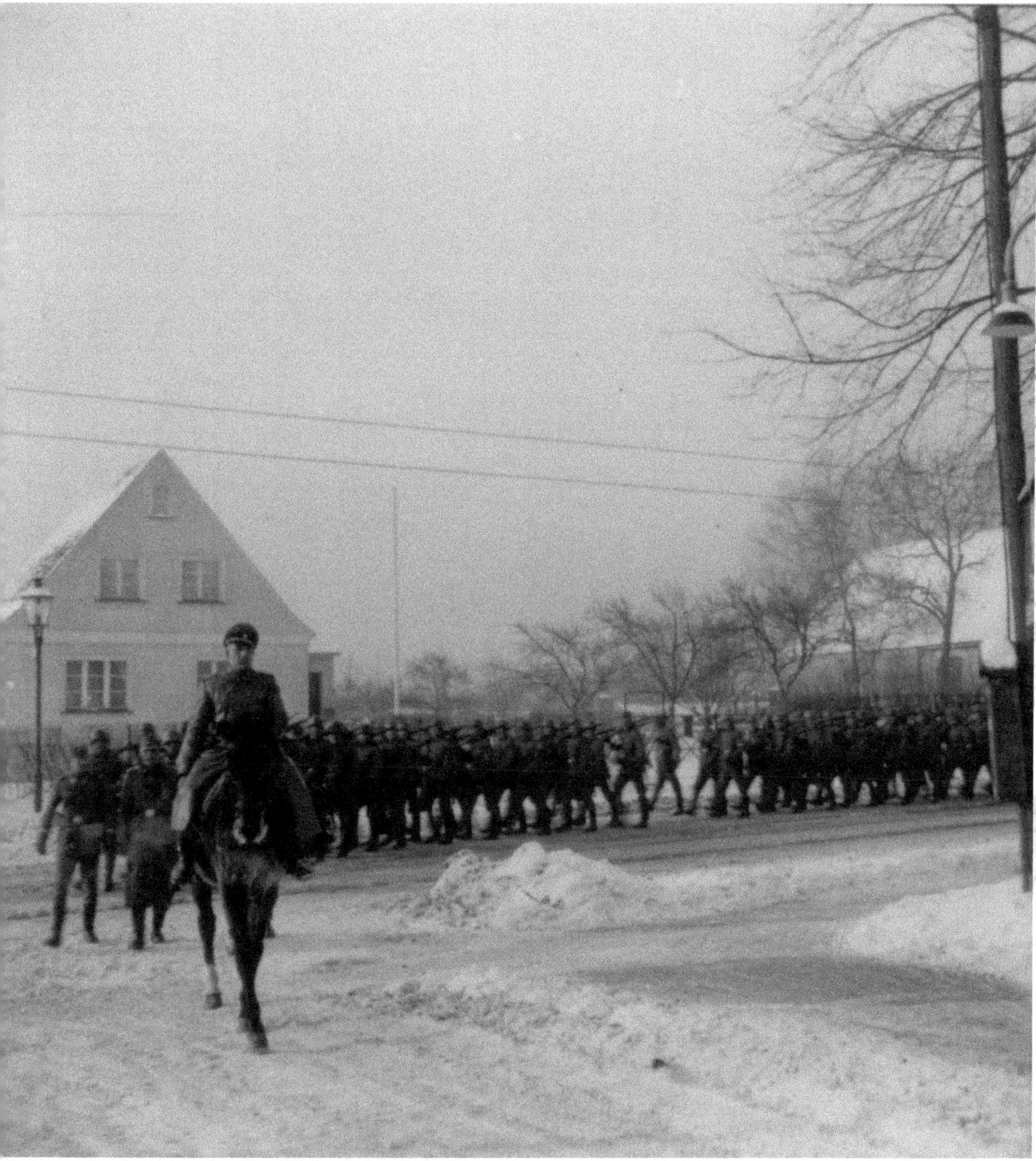

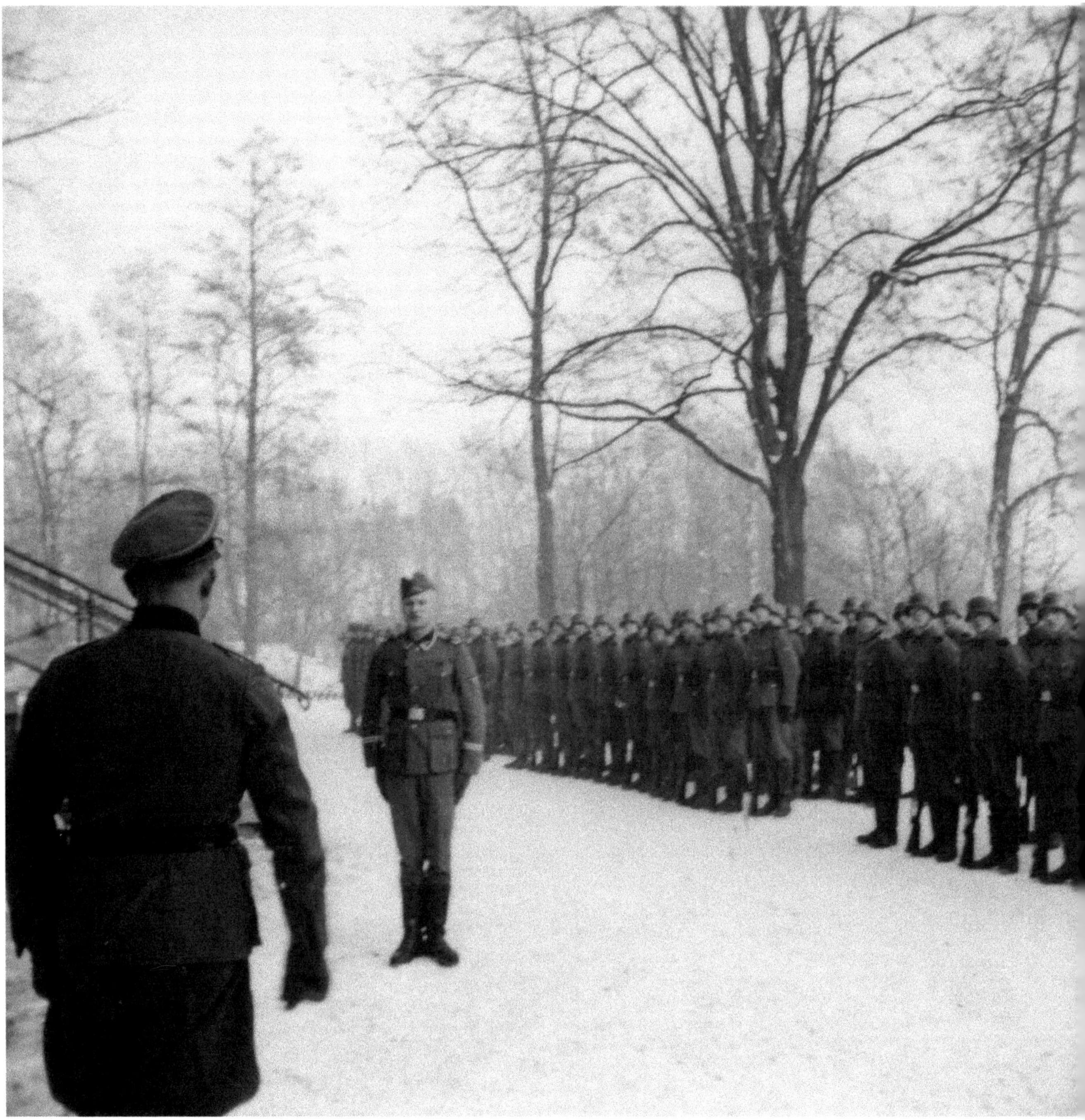

SS troops walking through iron gates to their barracks, accompanied by their commanding officer. There was a considerable difference between the attitudes of the SS and the rest of the armed services. While the Wehrmacht were to fight initially along the old military lines, the SS looked upon their service with a brutal attitude that knew no bounds. In many ways these troops found brutality to be the norm and often expressed this in the harsh and murderous activities against the Jews and anybody else regarded as hostile to their beliefs.

SS troops at a training ground during a passing-out ceremony bearing their oath to the Führer. Showing blind allegiance each soldier knew he was expected to step up and join one of the newly-created armed SS divisions where he would obey every order, even if it meant shooting prisoners and committing atrocities against civilians.

Chapter Two

The Low Countries, France and the Balkans

By the spring of 1940 the stage was set for war against the West. Distributed among the huge army poised to attack France and the Low Countries were two SS formations comprising the *Leibstandarte* and the SS-VT divisions. The *Totenkopf* ('Death's Head') and SS *Polizei* divisions were left in reserve. Among all the SS formations, the *Leibstandarte* and the SS-VT would play the most prominent part in the campaign.

The *Der Führer* Regiment of the SS-VT Division was organized into three regimental units, each of them consisting of three battalions with three infantry companies and one heavy company. The infantry companies were all motorized and armed with three light 5cm mortars, two heavy and nine light machine guns. The heavy weapons company consisted of six 8cm mortars and eight machine guns. Additionally in each of the regiments there were integrated five companies and platoons, which included a platoon of armoured cars, an anti-tank company with twelve 3.7cm PaK 36/35 guns and a motorcycle company. There was also a unit's band in each of the regiments. Incorporated into the division there were four combat units of battalion size comprising an anti-tank battalion with three companies of twelve 3.7cm PaK 35/36 guns in each of them, a reconnaissance battalion with two motorcycle companies that were armed with twenty-two machine guns and three light 5cm mortars, and a platoon of armoured cars used as the main fighting component. Pioneer and FlaK battalions were organized into three companies. The FlaK unit was armed with thirty-six heavy machine guns. The division was supported by standard supply troops with an artillery regiment consisting of three battalions, each of them comprising three batteries of twelve 10.5cm howitzers, all of which were motorized.

When Germany finally unleashed its military might on the West in May 1940, the SS-VT Division and the *Leibstandarte* crossed the Dutch border to join in the invasion of Holland. During the initial stages of the campaign the SS performed well and penetrated deep into enemy lines. Constantly and with great enthusiasm SS troops were seen leading furious attacks upon the bewildered Dutch troops, soon occupying the eastern end of Fortress Holland and pushing through the enemy lines, enabling 10th Corps to sweep past Utrecht and into the Dutch capital, Amsterdam. Although the *Der Führer* Regiment achieved noticeable success in Holland, the rest of the SS-*Verfügungs* Division did not see as much extensive action in the country.

During the early phase of the attack the main body of the division had been advancing in two motorized columns to Hilvarenbeek, a town north of Antwerp. Yet despite this slow start to the invasion the SS-*Verfügungs* Division soon secured German control over the western end of Holland. Meanwhile, *Heer* troops of Army Group B moved across into Belgium, captured Brussels, swept through Belgium and into northern France, and then began spearheading its powerful forces towards the English Channel.

As victory beckoned in Holland and Belgium, the SS *Totenkopf* Division was pulled out of reserve and ordered to exploit the enemy's deteriorating situation. Days later the SS *Polizei* Division, which was predominantly horse-drawn, was released from reserve and saw limited operations as it crossed the Aisne River and the Ardennes Canal. It was here that the latter became embroiled in heavy fighting against some stiff French opposition.

Elsewhere, while pockets of resistance fought to the bitter end, the Germans continued driving westward with all their might. On the evening of 22 May the SS-*Verfügungs* Division proceeded with the 6th and 8th Panzer divisions towards the port of Calais in order to help strengthen German positions west and south of the Dunkirk perimeter. It seemed that Dunkirk would soon be captured because on the night of 26 May Hitler rescinded his famous 'halt order' and *Germania* and *Der Führer* of the SS-*Verfügungs* Division surged back into action and fought a bloody battle in the Nieppe Forest. The remaining infantry regiment, *Deutschland*, which was temporarily attached to the 3rd Panzer Division, took part in the attack against British units on the Lys Canal near Merville where the SS troops met spirited resistance.

With the first phase of the war in the West completed, the Battle of France began. On 5 June 1940 German *Panzergruppen* attacked along the whole line. As elements of *Panzergruppe Kleist* steamrolled towards Paris, the *Leibstandarte* and the SS-*Verfügungs* Division joined the main drive. By the time the SS formations arrived on the outskirts of Paris, the French capital had been abandoned by its government. *Panzergruppe Kleist*, including the *Totenkopf*, *Leibstandarte* and the SS-*Verfügungs* Division, struck through Champagne towards Dijon in Burgundy to prevent the remnants of the French army retreating to the south-west of France.

By the end of June the campaign in the West was finally over and the SS troops returned to their home stations. However, late in 1940 the SS-*Verfügungs* Division returned to southern France and stationed in the town of Vesoul, being renamed the SS-*Deutschland* Division in December. A month later in January 1941 the name of the division was changed yet again and it became known as *Das Reich* (The Empire) Division (Motorized).

In March 1941 *Das Reich* Division, fully rearmed with more troops and equipment, was transported from southern France to south-west Romania. Within a month an order was received to attack Yugoslavia with the main objective of capturing the capital, Belgrade. It was left to *Das Reich* Division to take Belgrade, with hardly any resistance.

Following operations in Yugoslavia *Das Reich* Division returned to Romania and later moved to an area near Salzburg, Austria, for recuperation and a refit. During this period the division was reorganized. It consisted of the two SS regiments *Der Führer* and *Deutschland* but both were given three very strong battalions of motorized infantry regiments, comprising a motorized battery of artillery and platoons of motorcycle rifles, as well as armoured cars. The division had a very strong artillery regiment composed of four battalions with three companies in each. Additionally there were reconnaissance and anti-tank battalions armed with 3.7cm and 5cm anti-tank guns. To provide infantry support and increase anti-tank capability the division received a StuG.III battery .(organized in February) and a heavier armament for its anti-aircraft battalions. After 1 June the battalion was supported by twelve 8.8cm FlaK guns, which would become useful not only against air but also ground targets.

While *Das Reich* Division was reaping success in Yugoslavia, the *Leibstandarte* attacked from Bulgaria through Yugoslavia and then on to Greece. In the days that followed, the *Leibstandarte* outmanoeuvred and outfought their opponents until they captured the stronghold of Manastir near the Yugoslav-Greek border. At the Klidi Pass the SS were met by very firm resistance comprising British and Australian troops who were determined to hold the mountain crests that dominated the pass at all costs. However, the SS again demonstrated their skill and tenacity and fought a number of fierce unrelenting battles until they drove their brave enemy from their bombed and blasted defences.

Within days the SS drove forward against further resistance and cut off the remnants of the British forces. They went on and continued to drive retreating columns of confused enemy troops off the Metzovon Pass, thus sealing the fate of sixteen divisions of the Greek army. The ensuing days saw the SS in hot pursuit of retreating British forces, fleeing against fierce and determined attacks.

By 27 April German forces finally entered Athens, and before the end of the month the Germans were in full control of the country. The Balkan campaign for the SS was now at an end. Just before its victorious troops returned to barracks in Czechoslovakia to refit and prepare for their next campaign, units of the *Leibstandarte* were ordered to take part in another victory parade, this time in Athens.

The campaign in the Balkans had been a great triumph for the SS. Its great skill, élan and daring had brought about invincibility in the eyes of Hitler. As a consequence of its success and need for more troops, between 1941 and 1943 the Waffen-SS grew considerably. It also began conscripting ethnic Germans as well as suitably 'Nordic' volunteers (in keeping with the Aryan ideal). By 1943 many of the new divisions were predominantly manned by foreign soldiers with only about twelve of the divisions being regarded as true elite. However, this did not deter Hitler or Himmler from its expansion. They were confident that the SS, of whatever creed, would be led with the right leadership to ultimate victory.

While the expansion of the SS continued, in August 1943 Hitler ordered the transfer of his elite SS Panzer Corps from the Eastern Front to Italy following the Italian capitulation in July. This type of sudden shift became characteristic of the deployment of the elite SS divisions during the second half of the war, as Hitler used them as a 'fire brigade' to reinforce trouble spots. To help contain the advancing Anglo-American forces that had made an amphibious landing south of Rome at Anzio, the Waffen-SS were employed to stem the drive at all costs and fight to the death. As a result of the Italian campaign a number of Italian Waffen-SS formations were formed. Across Italy's endless mountain spine the Waffen-SS had many opportunities for a good defence. All through the Italian campaign the Germans enhanced this natural advantage by incorporating massive concrete emplacements and Panther tank turrets into their defensive lines which stretched across the vast hinterland of the Italian landscape.

As a result of the German defensive strategy, fighting in Italy proved very costly for both sides. While the Waffen-SS played little part in the conventional war in Italy, they were involved in the guerrilla campaign. Their actions, however, left an indelible mark on the Italian population. The SS were very brutal and mass killings were quite common. Throughout the Italian campaign these forces proved as barbaric as they had been on the Eastern Front.

SS troops continued to fight alongside their *Heer* counterparts and continued to stand and fight for every river line as they slowly retreated towards the Austrian border. While the SS fought and murdered their way through Italy, in northern France Waffen-SS divisions were preparing themselves for an invasion of mainland Europe.

A medium Auto-Union/Horch (probably a Kfz.11) belonging to a *Das Reich* reconnaissance battalion with a full complement of crew. Note the national flag draped over the vehicle's engine cover for aerial recognition purposes. Of interest are the two French bayonets attached to the front of the vehicle's radiator.

A heavy MG34 machine-gun section belonging to *Das Reich* have set up their MG on a tripod mount. The MG34 was an excellent general purpose weapon and along the front lines enemy soldiers had great respect for the German machine guns and their highly-trained crews.

A PaK 35/36 team of the 2nd SS Regiment *Germania* preparing their anti-tank gun for action. The weapon's splinter shield is well-camouflaged with foliage. Note the ammunition carrier and the ammunition box with an inscription painted in white which reads: 'Pat. 3.7cm PaK' – Rounds [Patronen] 3.7cm anti-tank gun. Two of the soldiers are standing on the gun's trail spades in order to prevent the gun from recoiling backwards too far as it fires on a cobbled road on which the trail spades cannot fullly embed themselves into the ground.

A motorcycle pioneer platoon from an unidentified regiment belonging to *Das Reich* removing mines from a road. The soldier in the background watching the work being carried out is equipped with a knapsack mine-detector which was still a very rare piece of equipment at the time. Note the NCO in the foreground armed with a 9mm Bergmann MP28 machine pistol which was mainly issued to troop commanders in the field.

A *Das Reich* PaK 35/36 crew guards the approaches of a road in a town in northern France. The PaK 35/36 became the standard anti-tank weapon in both the *Heer* and Waffen-SS during the early part of the war. It weighed only 432kg and had a sloping splinter shield that afforded minimal protection to the crew.

A heavy weapons section from a *Das Reich* regiment is preparing to cross a river on a 6-metre medium pneumatic boat. The first soldier to step on board is carrying a variety of equipment including an 8cm mortar ammunition box and rangefinder. The other two troops are bringing on board the mortar base-plate and a folded mortar mount.

A motorcyclist poses for the camera with his motorcycle on the side of a road in May 1940. This soldier belongs to an unidentified *Totenkopf* unit while in reserve during the Western campaign. The soldier holds the rank of an SS-*Rottenführer* or section leader. Note the death's head insignia painted either in white or yellow on the 15cm siG33 artillery gun shield.

SS troops on the march through a French town in June 1940. These men more than likely belong to the SS *Polizei* Division, which was predominantly horse drawn. While it was recognized even at this early stage of the war that horses were slow and it took time to move artillery pieces around the battlefield and considerable time to achieve fire-readiness, in France much of the work had already been accomplished by tracked vehicles. The inadequacy of horse drawn vehicles would be grimly demonstrated in the Russian campaign.

A column of horse-drawn transport belonging to the SS *Polizei* Division. The horses are towing the 10.5cm field howitzer. It was primarily these artillery regiments that were given the task of destroying enemy positions and conducting counter-battery fire prior to an armoured assault. Throughout the war this weapon provided both the *Heer* and SS divisions with a versatile, relatively mobile base of fire.

SS artillery crew pause at the side of the road with their halted column somewhere in France in June 1940.

The following eight photographs showing the same SS battery in France. Combat experience showed that artillery support was of decisive importance in both defensive and offensive roles. In total the 10.5cm howitzer had a nine-man crew. Usually fewer are seen serving this piece because often some of the crew were to the rear with the horses, limber and caisson. The 10.5cm light field howitzer was used extensively during the first half of the war. Although these howitzers provided armour-piercing and shaped-charged anti-tank rounds, the guns were far from being effective anti-tank weapons. In one of the photographs a number of propellant charges and 10.5cm ammunition charges can be seen laid out, showing the gun being readied and fired against an enemy target. The rate of fire was four to six rounds per minute.

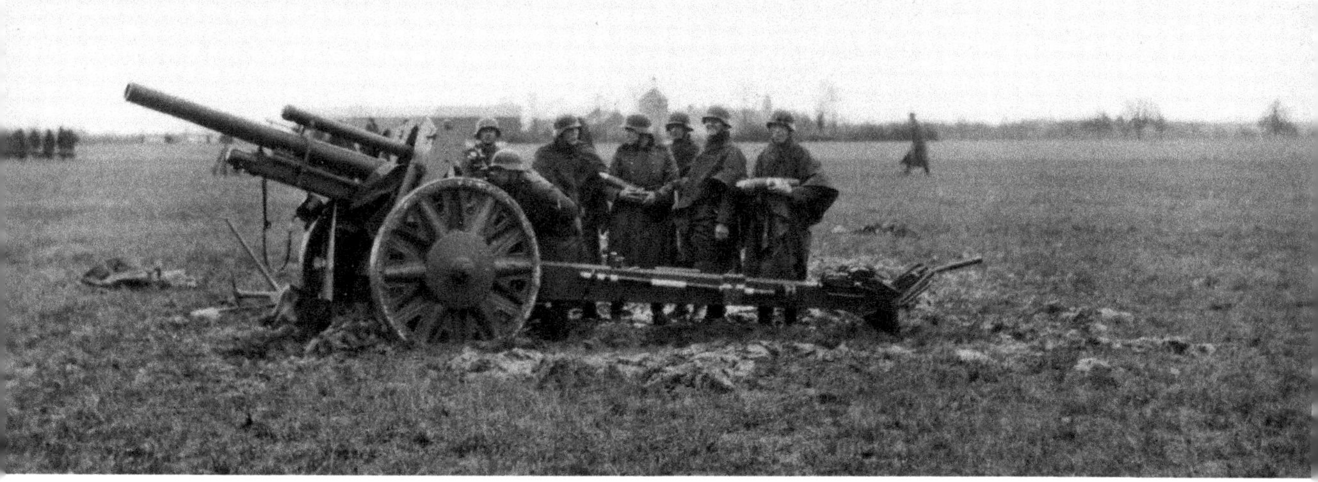

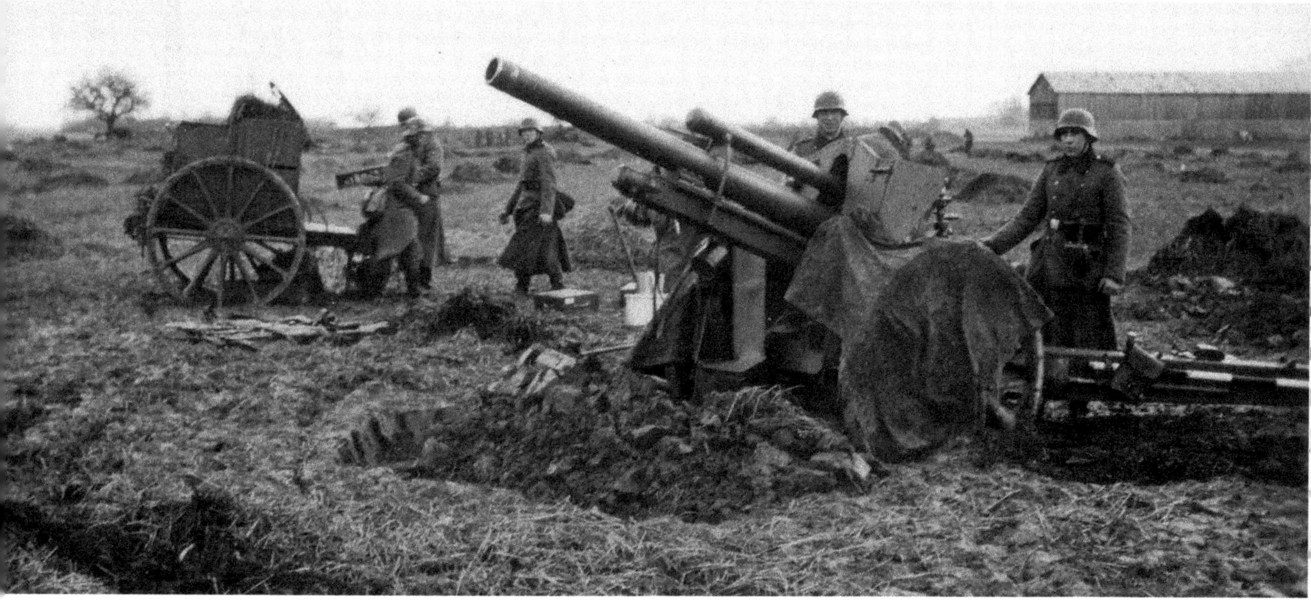

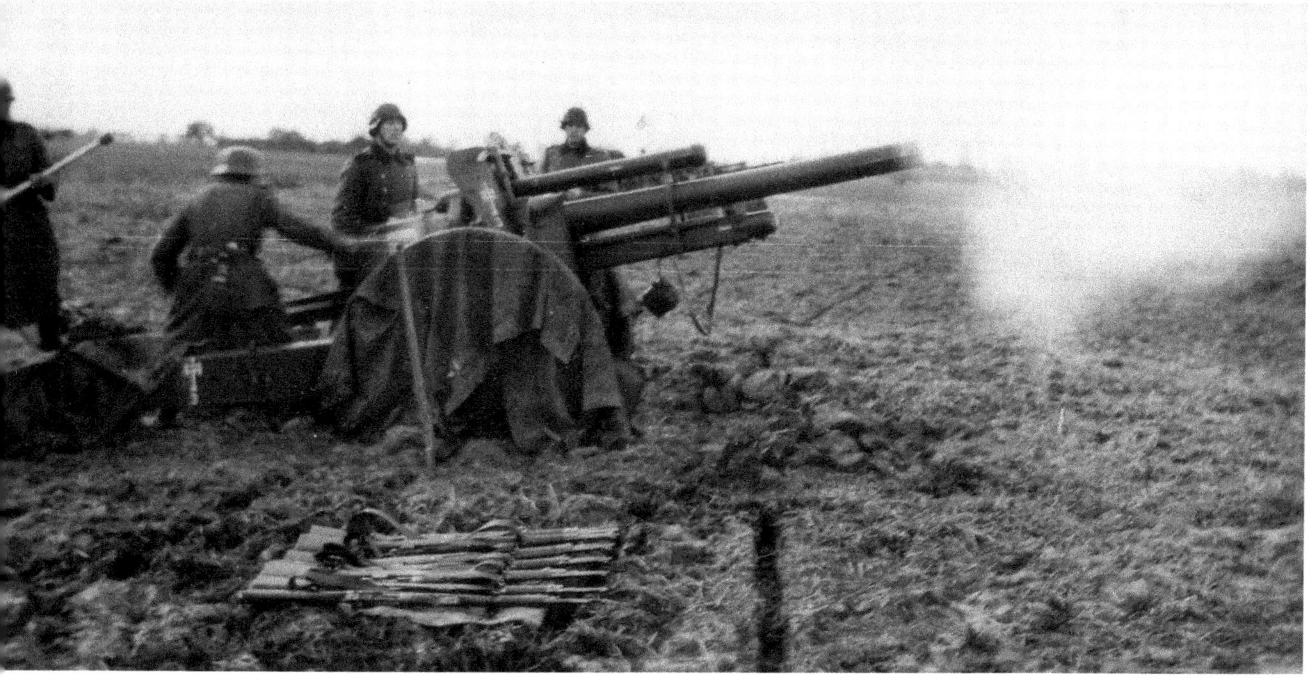

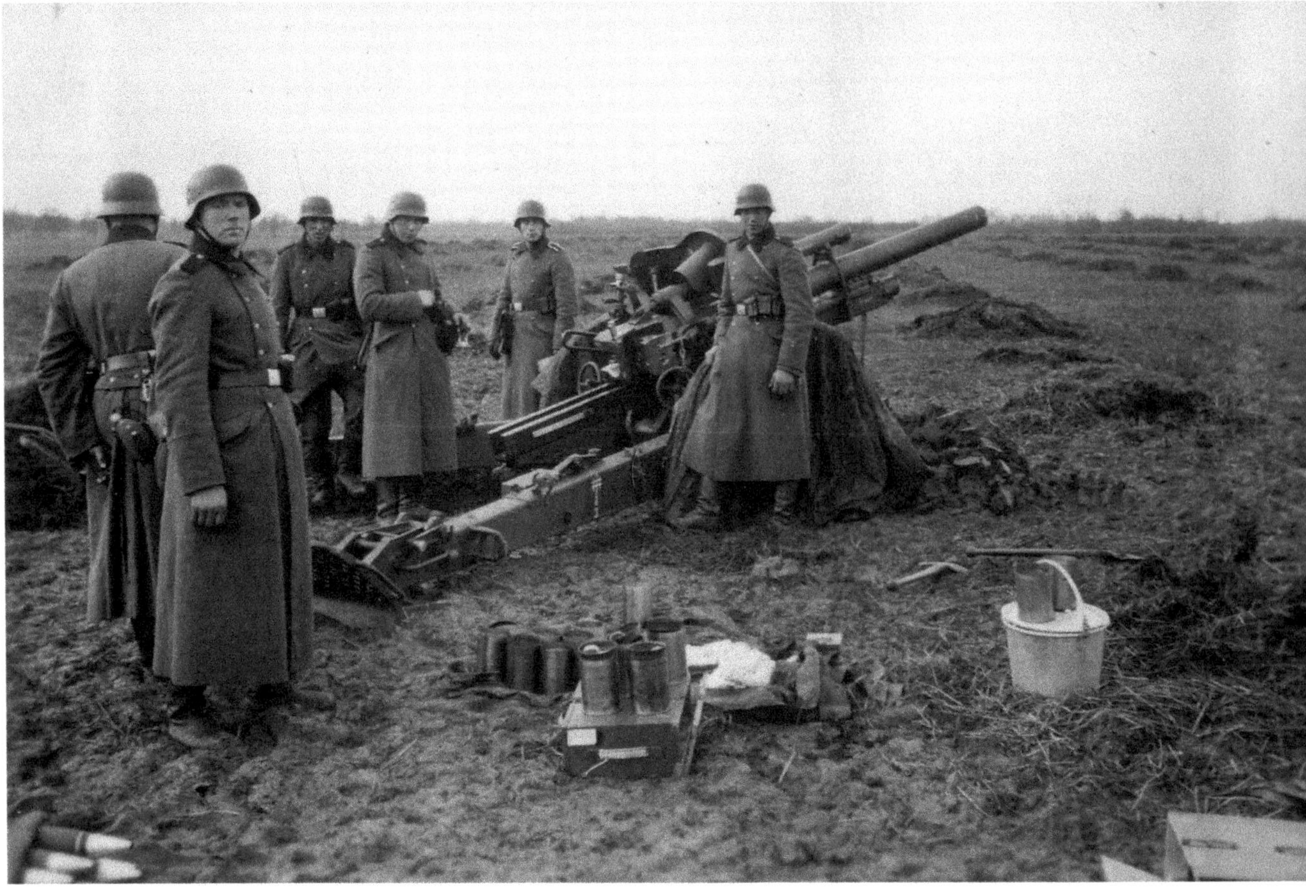

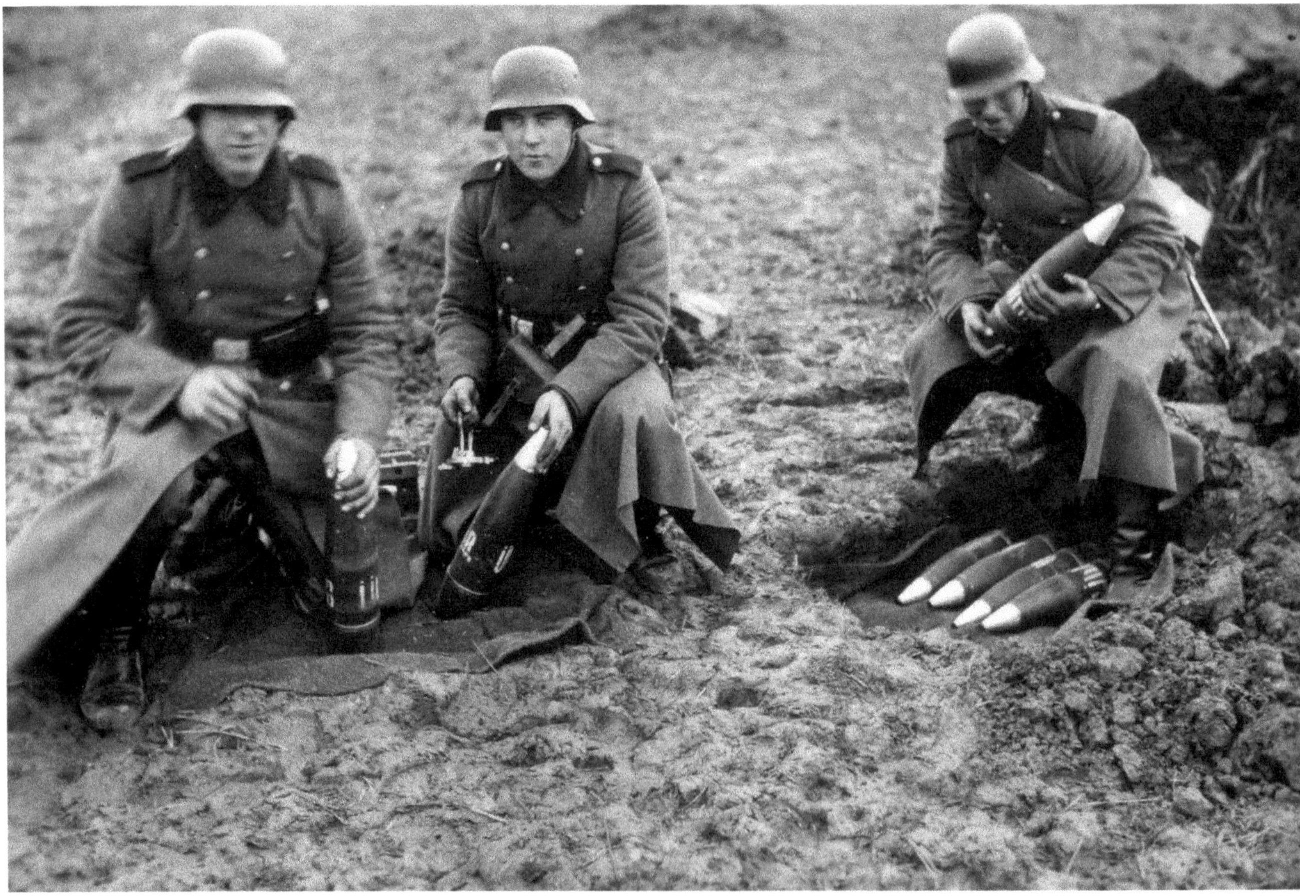

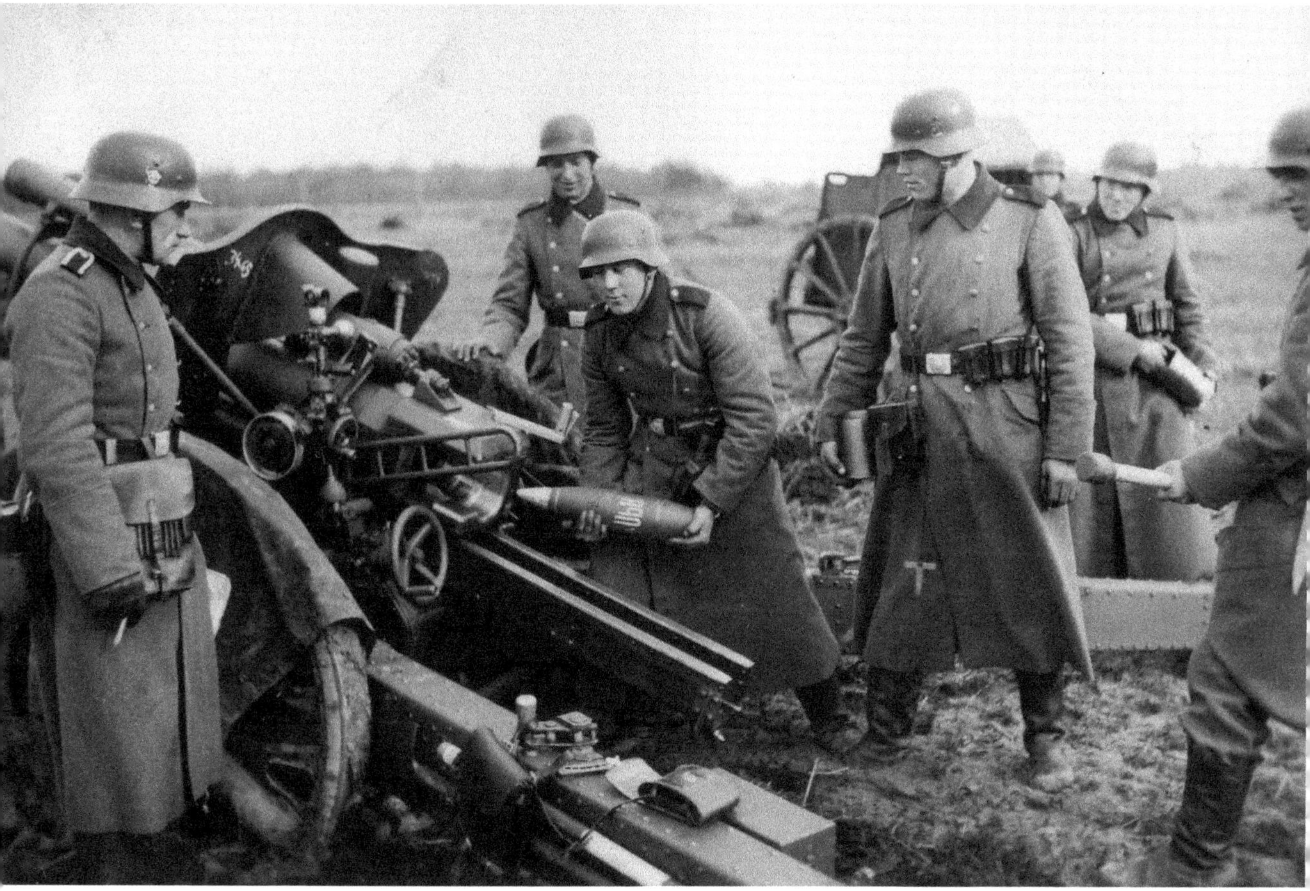

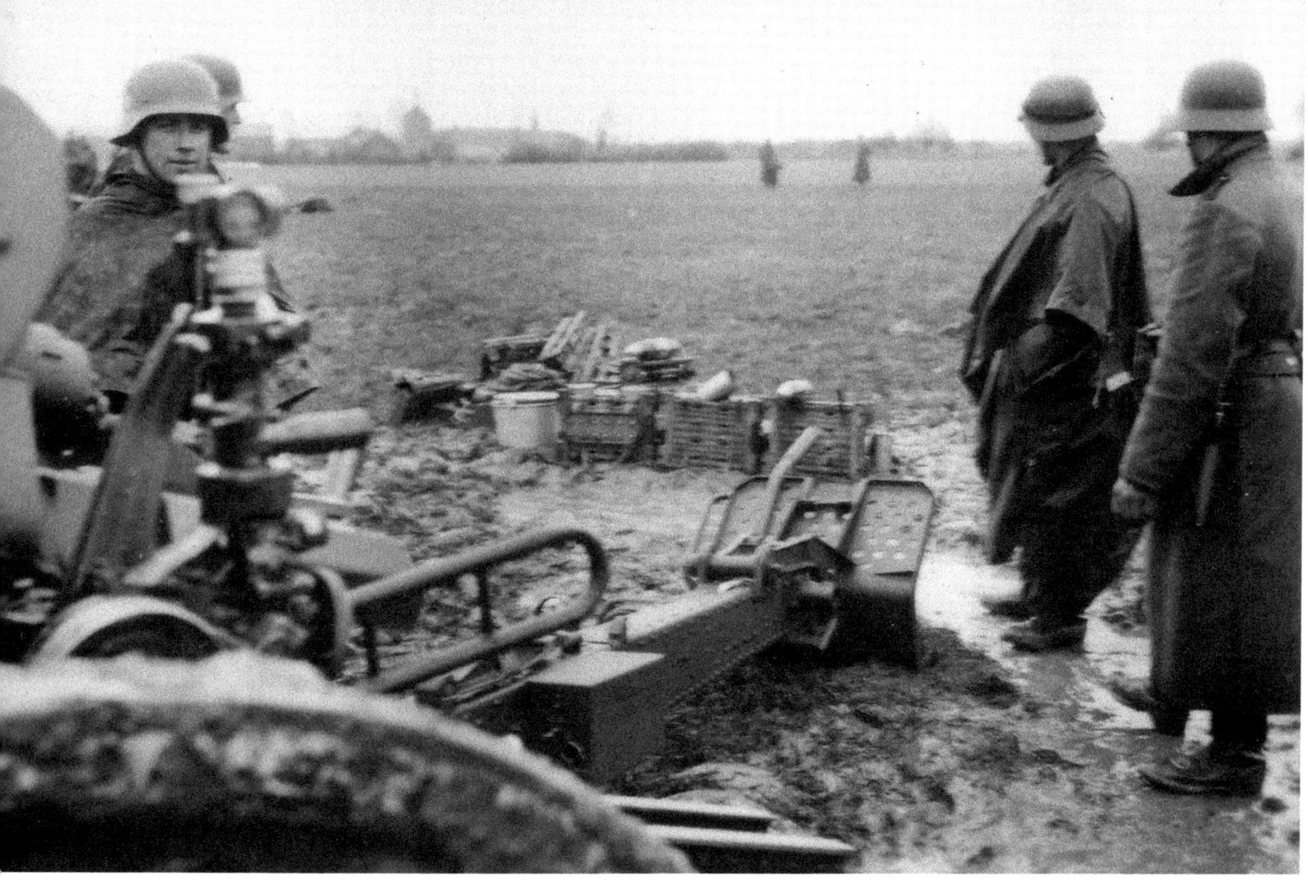

During the Western campaign and an SS mortar group can be seen with their 8cm sGrW 34 mortar in action against an enemy target. Each battalion fielded six of these excellent mortars, which could fire fifteen bombs per minute to a range of 2,625 yards.

Four SS soldiers, two holding the rank of SS-*Hauptsturmführer* (senior storm leader), one SS-*Truppführer* (troop leader), and an SS-*Mann* (trooper) survey the battlefield with the aid of notes. They are all wearing their summer camouflage uniforms.

SS troops advancing along a forest track during the campaign in the West. By the end of the first day of the attack against the West, Belgian resistance had been overwhelmed and the cavalry of the French 9th Army brushed aside. Although the French 7th Army had reached Breda on 11 May, by the next day it was in retreat under strong pressure from Guderian's Panzers. By the evening of that same day the Panzer units reached the Meuse along a 100-mile front, from Sedan to Dinant.

Troops of the SS *Polizei* Division in a French town waiting to be called into action. The division was formed in 1939 as part of the *Ordnungspolizei* or *Orpo* (paramilitary police). The formation during this early period of its transformation from police unit to a fighting force was basically an infantry division. It was primarily horse-drawn and initially held in reserve with Army Group C in the Rhineland during the Battle of France until 9 June when it first saw combat during the crossing of the Aisne river and the Ardennes Canal.

Two photographs showing *Totenkopf* troops on the march westwards to the Belgian border on 12 May 1940. The division waited another four days before being committed to battle. They were assigned to Army Group A and were given plans to strike across southern Holland, through Belgium and into France to link up with General Hoth's 15th Panzer-Korps.

Troops of the *Polizei* Division during a lull in the fighting can be seen resting inside a bombed French town in June 1940. Although officially formed under the arm of the SS, the *Polizei* was not technically an SS division at this time as it was mainly comprised of older national police personnel. Unlike the other divisions such as the *Leibstandarte*, *Das Reich* and *Totenkopf*, the *Polizei* was regarded as a second-rate SS unit and was not fully motorized. Instead of standard SS equipment, the division was mainly supplied with antiquated and captured hardware.

Soldiers of the *Polizei* Division resting in the ruins of a destroyed French town, which by the appearance of the buildings has received both heavy ground and aerial shelling. When this division was finally released for action in France it was untried in battle. Its members were considerably older than other SS men and their lack of training and poor equipment hardly helped to inspire the confidence of their *Heer* counterparts either.

A group of SS troops pose for the camera during a pause in their advance. Note the requisitioned bus that has been utilized to carry troops to the front. Foliage has been draped over the roof of the vehicle due to the threat of an aerial attack. Behind the bus is a very long column of trucks carrying men and matériel to the front. The German spearhead through Belgium and Holland was swift and within days the British were facing the prospect of losing their only army and entire parts of their air force if they continued to stand by their allies on a collapsing battle line. The French too were under incredible pressure from the German onslaught and foresaw their army breaking in two, with the stronger part falling victim to the encirclement in Belgium and areas in the north. It was now decided that in order to save their forces from complete destruction, the BEF would have to make a fighting withdrawal into northern France and hopefully stave off a catastrophe there.

Two SS troops have their photograph taken among the carnage that was wrought in one of the many towns and villages that lay under the German spearheads. By 18 May 1940 Panzers were reportedly sweeping on into France. By 20 May, after racing north along the Somme against fierce resistance from the British 12th and 23rd (Territorial) divisions, the first Panzers came in sight of the Channel coast. In no more than eleven days Guderian and his force had advanced 400 miles and done what the German army failed to accomplish in four years during the First World War. It seemed nothing on earth could stop this stampede of military might from crushing the Anglo-French troops that were being driven along the Channel coast.

(*Facing page*) Three photographs taken in sequence showing troops of the 1st *Totenkopf* Infantry Regiment with a handful of captured Moroccan soldiers in the Cambrai region of France. It was in this area that the *Totenkopf* managed to capture 16,000 prisoners and a large amount of battlefield booty. During this battle the SS saw its first casualties of combat when French and Moroccan forces fought a fierce defensive action. Only 100 Moroccan troops were captured. Most of the surrendering Africans were simply shot out of hand, being regarded by the Germans as 'sub-human'. While one of the SS officers can be seen laughing with the Moroccans, it is highly likely that these captured men would have been murdered sometime after this photograph was taken. The *Totenkopf* were the worst offenders but all the front-line SS divisions committed similar atrocities.

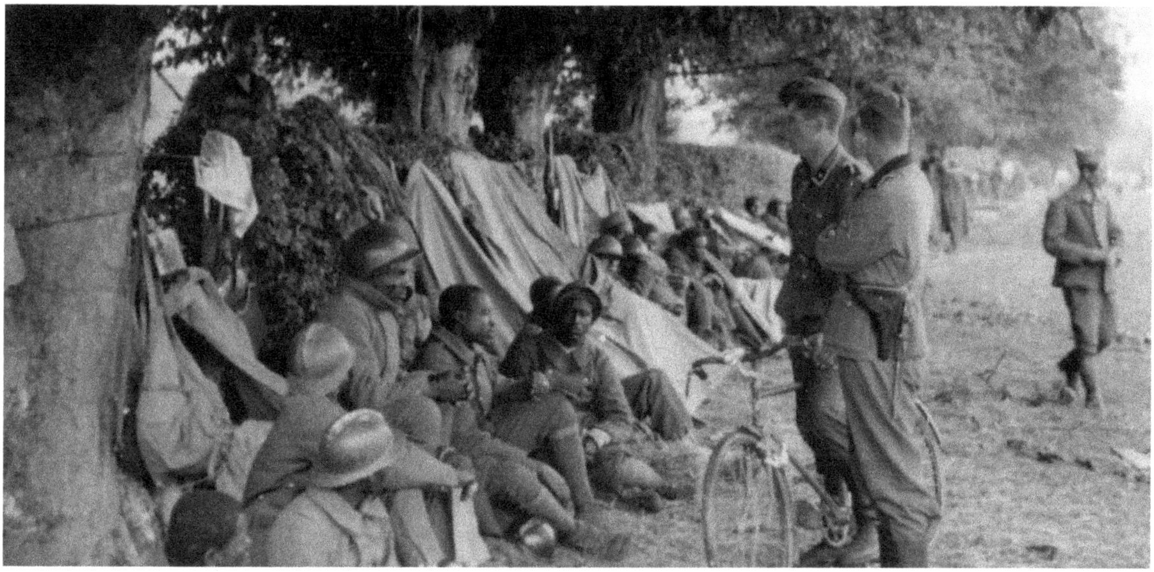

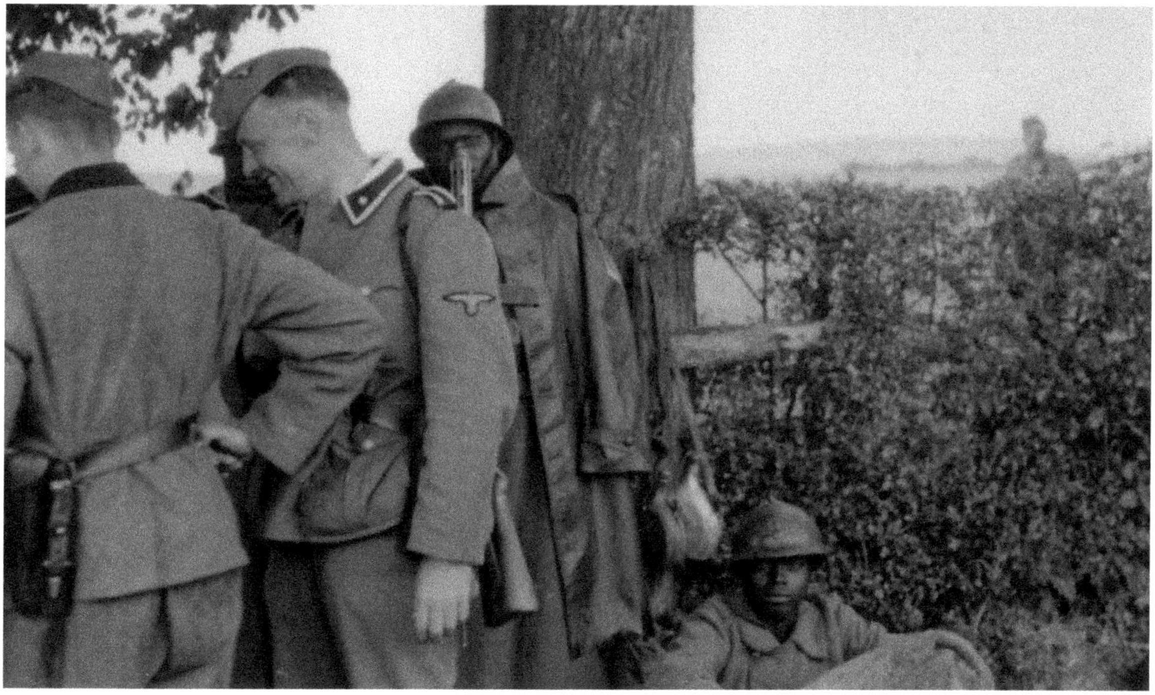

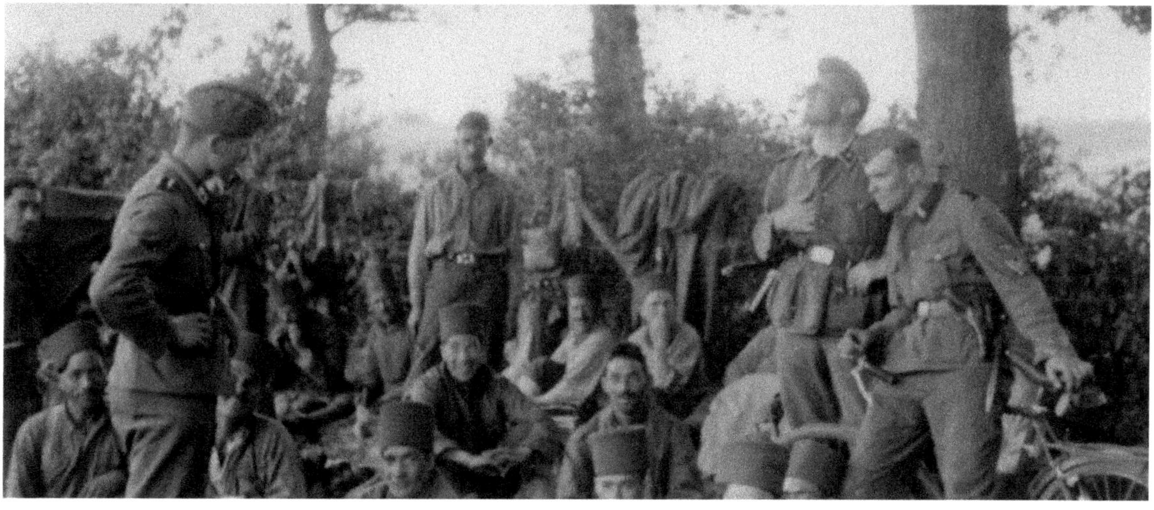

An SS heavy MG34 machine-gun position. This machine gun could inflict terrible losses on an advancing enemy. Throughout the Western campaign and indeed for the rest of the war the MG34 had tremendous stopping power against enemy infantry, and troops continuously deployed their machine guns in the most advantageous defensive and offensive positions.

A column of vehicles belonging to the *Totenkopf* Division has halted in a French town. The German drive through France was undertaken effectively and efficiently. In a number of areas German tank commanders reported that the enemy was simply brushed aside, thrown into complete confusion. In most cases the defenders lacked any force capable of mounting a strong coordinated counter-attack. British artillery, struggling with very limited ammunition supplies to stem the German onslaught, soon found that the enemy was too strong to be halted for any appreciable length of time.

Posing for the camera these *Totenkopf* troops are seen relaxing in front of a First World War monument. By 14 June 1940 the *Totenkopf* had joined *Das Reich*, *Leibstandarte* and the *Polizei* Division in the pursuit of what was left of the French army and their allies. The French and British forces tried in vain to regain the initiative, and a catastrophe now threatened the Allied armies.

Luftwaffe, *Heer* and SS troops together during a lull in the fighting. The quality of the German weapons was of immense importance to the success in France. German tactics were the best and its troops' stubborn defence, concentrated local firepower from machine guns and mortars, and rapid counter-attacks to recover lost ground were significant. German units often fought on even when cut off, which was not a mark of fanaticism but great tactical discipline. The invasion of the Low Countries and France was a product of great organization and staff work, and marvellous technical ingenuity. Note the Opel Blitz lorries.

Totenkopf on the move along a French road. SS infantry can be seen in the field next to an abandoned French Renault R-35 light tank. By the second week of June 1940 militarily the French were doomed. Demoralized by increasing losses, troops and commanders in the field became infected with defeatism. Their armies were in pitiful shape. They had been broken up, their armour expended and little was left of the weak air force. Nevertheless, some French units continued to fight with great bravery and tenacity, temporarily stopping even German armour and standing up resolutely to the incessant bombing of the Luftwaffe. But it was an unequal struggle. Note the white visibility markings painted on the rear of the lorry for safer night time driving.

Three photographs taken showing the graves of fallen SS soldiers. Much was made of the SS killed in action and funerals were tailored to suit Nazi ideology, particularly SS Heinrich Himmler's notions about the fallen warrior of the Aryan-Nordic race. To him, the SS soldier was an example of the new Aryan man, and if the 'warrior' was to be sacrificed on the battlefield, he was to be honoured as a hero of the 'Black Order'.

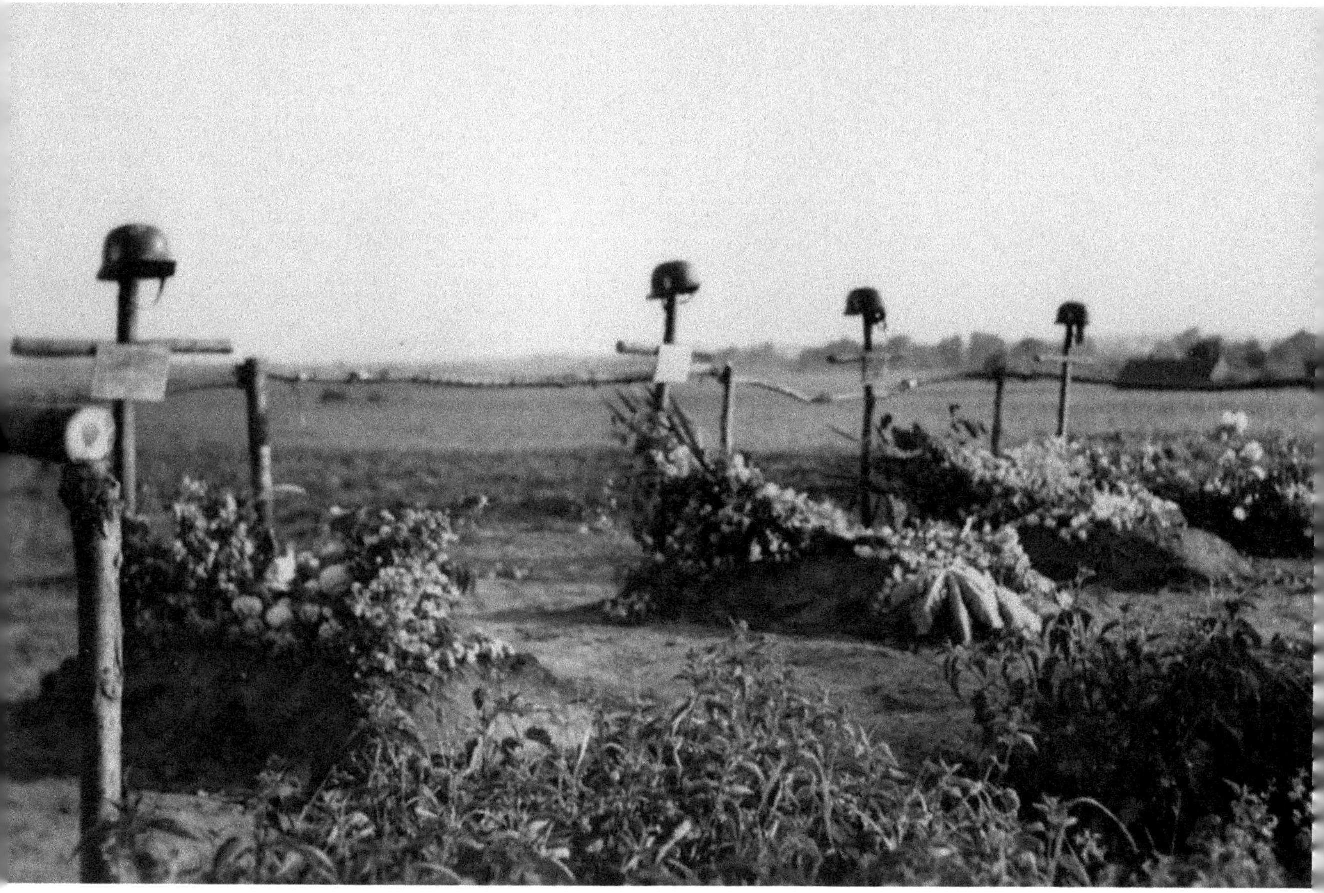

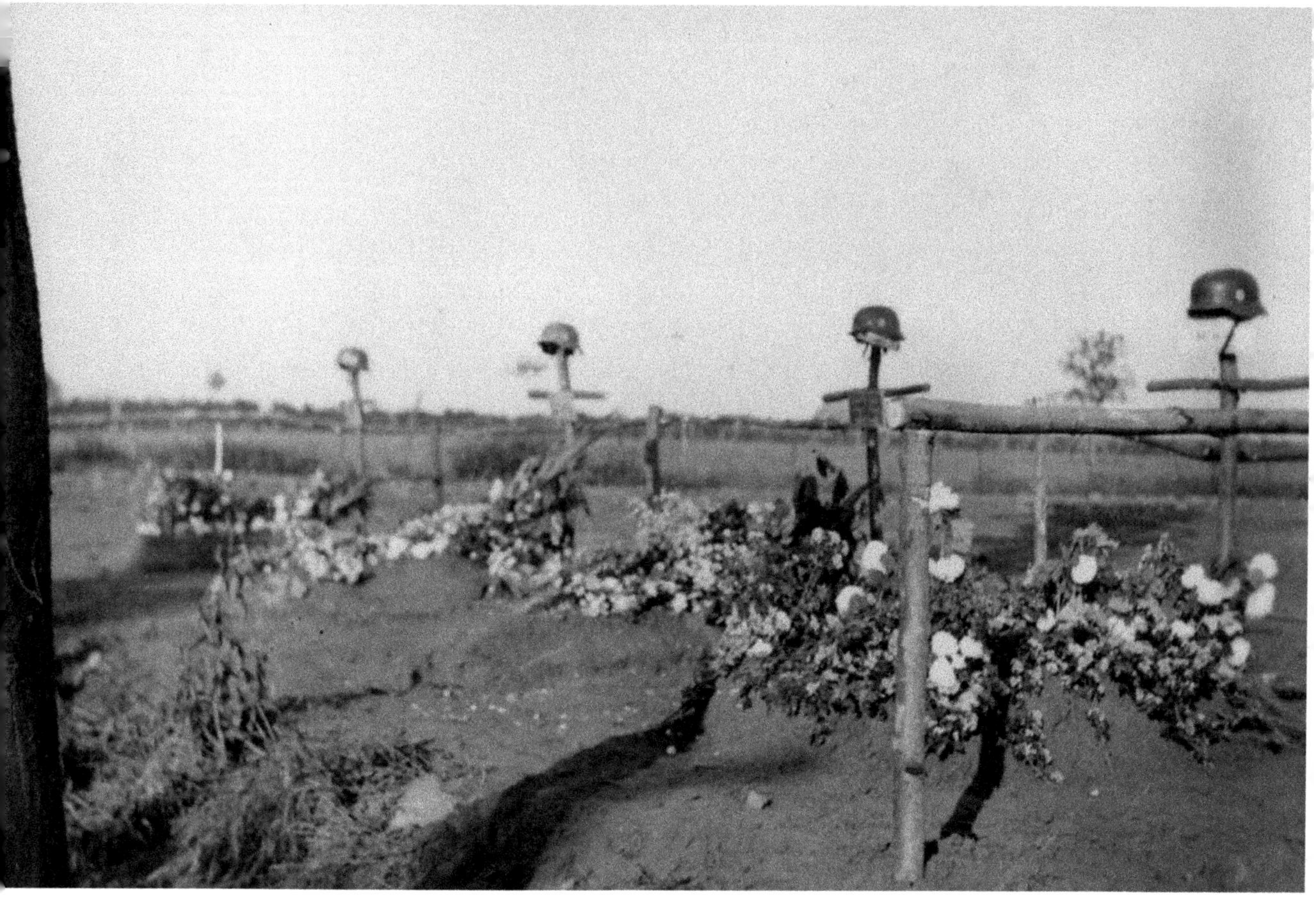

More than likely a posed shot showing an old *Maschinengewehr* 08 or MG08 being used in an anti-aircraft role. This was the German army's standard machine gun during the First World War. The MG08 remained in service until the outbreak of the Second World War due to shortages of its successors, the MG13 Dreyse and the MG34. It was retired from front-line service by 1942.

An SS Opel Blitz supply truck passes across a typical pontoon bridge erected across one of the many rivers that stretched through the Low Countries and north-eastern France. First engineers would position the pontoon boats (either inflatable or 50-ft pontoon boats) in place and then the bridging equipment would be erected across it in a surprisingly short time. Some of the pontoon boats were fitted with large outboard motors to hold the bridge sections in place against the often strong currents. However, because there were so many waterways that needed to be crossed by so many different divisions, the Germans found that they were running out of bridging equipment.

In a large field spread out as far as the eye can see is a troop encampment erected by the *Polizei* Division during its employment in the West in 1940. Note the number of horses and horse-drawn transports. Because the division was not motorized it had to rely heavily on draught animals. Often the troops found forested areas such as the Ardennes quite challenging. A year later the division would be issued with a number of tracked vehicles in order to overcome the problem of moving men, equipment and horses over difficult terrain.

An Opel Blitz lorry has halted on a French road. This truck is carrying *Totenkopf* troops. Foliage has been applied to the vehicle in order to minimize the threat of an aerial attack. Rolled netting can also be seen, which was used when the vehicle was stationary for any length of time.

SS troops on the march along a road littered with the carnage of a fleeing enemy. Bloated dead horses caught in the fighting are a grim reminder of war. By mid-June 1940 the French were unable to cope with the rapid speed at which events were constantly unfolding. There was nothing cowardly about the performance of the French army: it was simply overcome by the German tactics of Blitzkrieg. Faced with the total collapse of their army, the French continued to display sacrificial courage, despite high casualties.

Four photographs showing tanks and other vehicles of an unidentified French armoured unit abandoned in a town. Refugees can be seen fleeing from the front as German troops examine the Renault R-35 tanks (on the right) and a Hotchkiss H-35 tank (on the left). The R-35 was used extensively during the battle for France. It was armed with a 37mm short gun and crewed by two men. All along the German front a succession of large and small-scale actions took place, driving vital wedges into the French defences. French strongpoints were being knocked out, either by vigorous gunfire from Panzers or by determined action from *Heer* and SS infantry. The French army was now being swamped by scores of German units who succeeded almost everywhere.

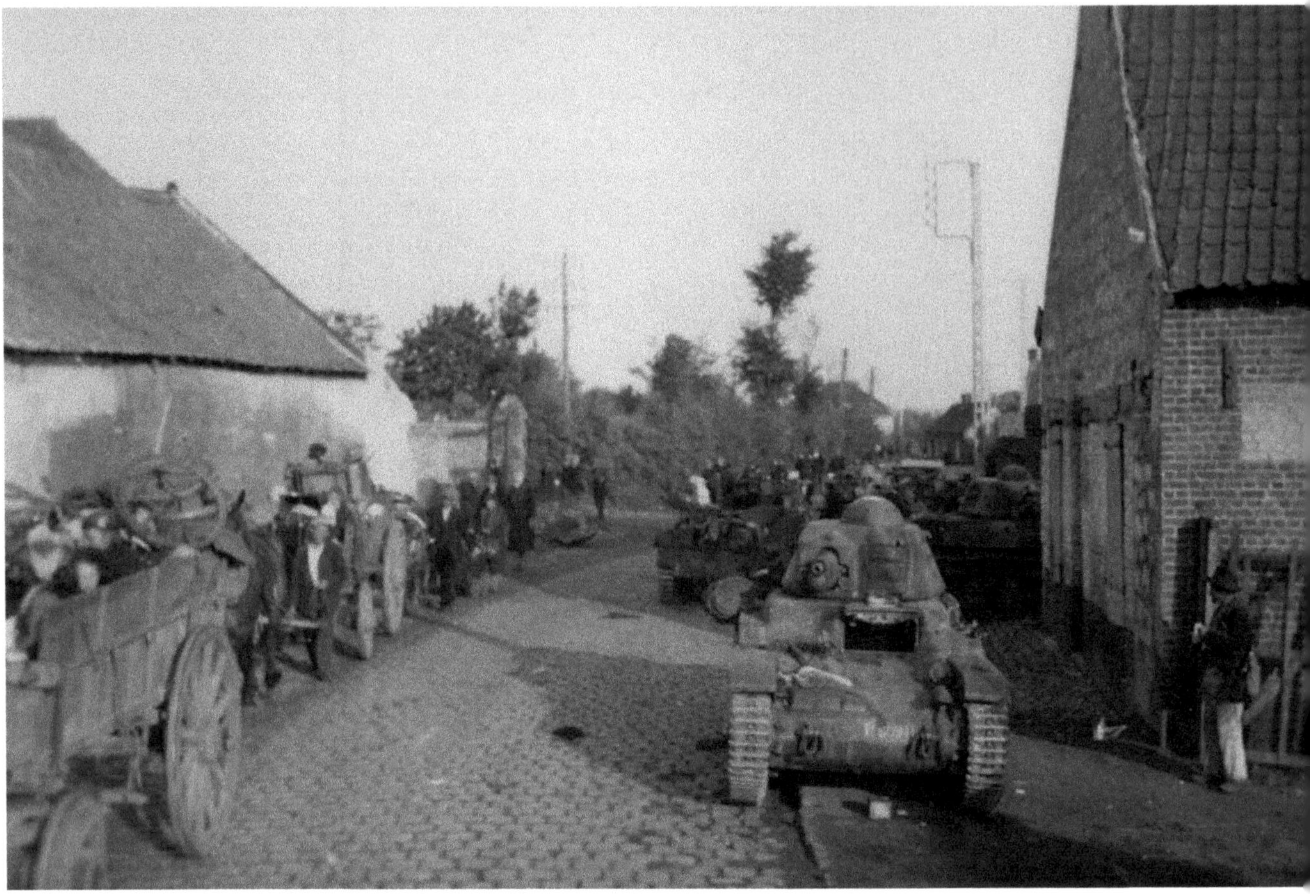

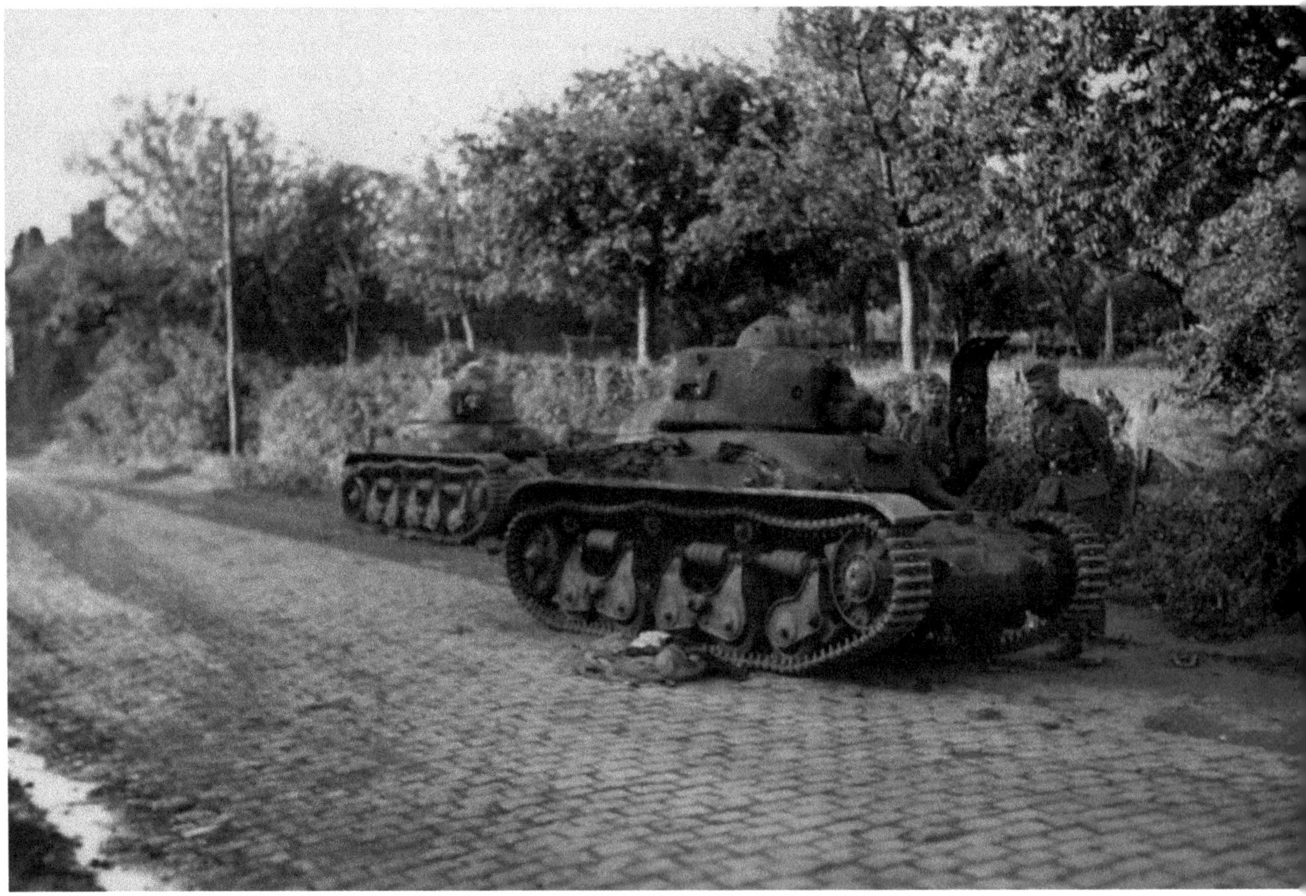

German troops belonging to *Das Reich* move through a badly damaged French town during the last days of the war in the West in June 1940. Note the column of Opel Blitz light trucks. These vehicles were specially designed to carry at least a squad of twelve men including their personal equipment and infantry weapons to the front lines.

A *Das Reich* staff vehicle and motorcycle can be seen pulled up in a destroyed French town during operations in northern France in June 1940. The staff car registration number plate is SS-10251. Note the vehicle number 14 painted on the mudguard, just under the registration plate.

Schwerer Panzerspähwagen (Funk) or heavy armoured reconnaissance vehicle (radio) Sd.Kfz.232. This was the command link version of the standard heavy armoured reconnaissance vehicle, designed to radio back information rather than to fight, in keeping with standard German doctrine. It was fitted with the Fu. Ger.11 SE 100 medium-range radio and a Fu. Spr. Ger. short-range radio. For local defence it was armed with a 2cm KwK 30 L/55 cannon.

Totenkopf troops pose for the camera next to a motorcycle combination. Note the motorcyclist wearing the motorcycle waterproof coat, which was issued to members of both the *Heer* and SS motorcycle units and individual motorcyclists. This coat was a double-breasted rubberized item of clothing. It was made of cotton twill coated rubber with watertight seams and was worn over the service uniform. The coat was loose-fitting and the ends of the garment could be easily gathered in around the wearer's legs and buttoned into position, which allowed easier and safer movement while riding the motorcycle. The motorcycle coat was grey-green in colour and had a woollen field-grey material collar and large pockets. When in use the wearer normally wore the army canvas and leather issue gloves or mittens. Normal leather army boots were often worn. Insignia was not officially worn with the coat but NCOs and officers were sometimes seen attaching their uniform straps. However, without shoulder straps, which was normally the case, the wearer's rank could seldom be identified. When required, the wearer generally wore his personal equipment over his rubberized coat including the gas mask canister and gas cape. The motorcycle coat was a popular, practical and very durable piece of protective clothing and was worn throughout the war. It was so popular that even infantrymen were sometimes seen wearing the coats and would adapt the garment by cutting it short to the knee and removing the wrist straps. Although this allowed for ease of movement, it reduced durability and the garment quickly became shabby and torn.

Totenkopf troops watch the endless columns of French refugees moving along a congested road. They pass a column of stationary Opel Blitz supply trucks which are destined for the front lines.

An SS soldier can just be seen among thick vegetation. A light Horch cross-country vehicle can also be made out, hidden in the foliage in order to avoid enemy aerial detection. The vehicle's SS licence plate can just be recognized.

Totenkopf MG troops are seen cleaning the 7.9mm barrel of a MG34 machine gun. To ensure the effective fire of the weapon it was imperative that the barrel and the rest of the gun were free from any grime or dirt. One soldier can be seen standing next to the sustained fire mount for the machine gun. Note the special pads on the front of the tripod. These were specifically used when the weapon was being borne on the carrier's back, allowing him some reasonable comfort.

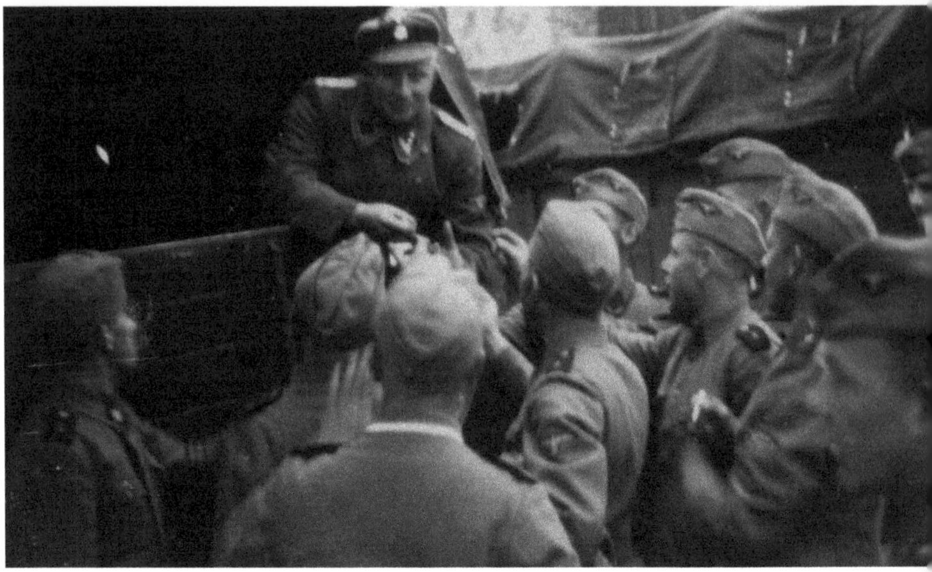

A *Totenkopf* commanding officer is handing something out to his troops from the rear of an infantry supply truck.

A battery of 10.5cm le.FH18 howitzers in their firing position in a field being readied for action. Normally there were four guns in a battery but sometimes, depending on losses or the strength of the enemy, the units were consolidated into slightly larger batteries. In total the 10.5cm howitzer had either an eight- or nine-man crew. Note the special wicker cases for the projectiles, a number of which have already been primed by the crew for firing. The 10.5cm howitzer had a good reputation on the battlefield. It was a reliable and stable weapon and crews found it easy to manoeuvre from one part of the front to another. On the Western Front the German infantry artillery formed the main organic support of the division and supported the combat troops prior to and during action. It was of paramount importance that these infantry field guns used on the battlefield were light and manoeuvrable. The 10.5cm light infantry gun was the ideal weapon for action on the front lines and undertook sterling service against the BEF.

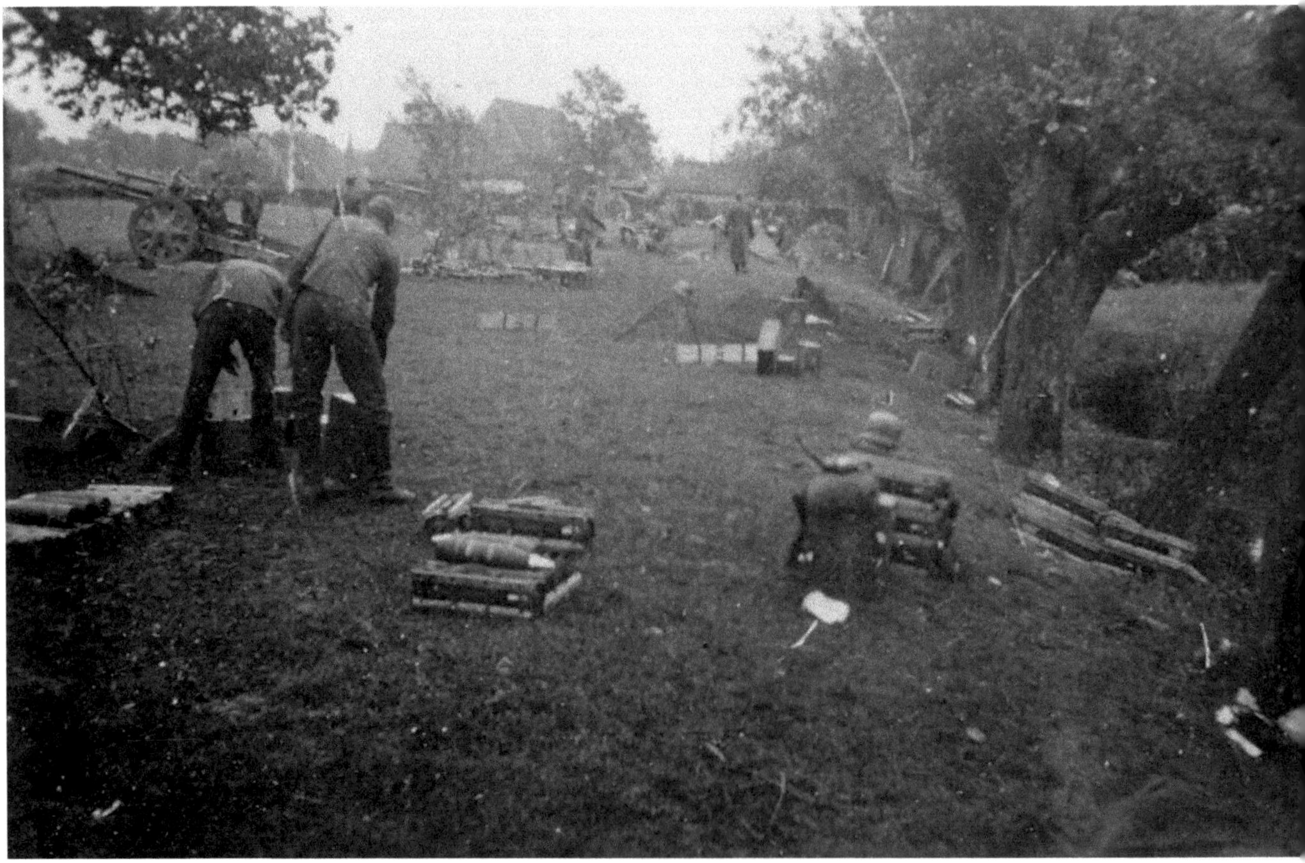

Two photographs taken by *Das Reich* showing a long column of French PoWs being escorted along a road to the rear, passing the division's motirized infantry and supporting vehicles. The lorries are Opel Blitz type. In the final days just before the French army capitulated, the Germans continued their advance. By 20 June it was estimated that some 500,000 French soldiers had been captured. Large amounts of battlefield booty also fell into German hands. By the end of the campaign some 94,000 French soldiers had been killed in the battle for France and about a quarter of million injured. Almost 2 million French soldiers were taken prisoner by the Germans. By contrast, the German losses were much smaller, with 27,000 dead and 111, 000 wounded.

By 14 June the first German troops from the 9th Infantry Division reported that they had arrived on the outskirts of Paris. Later that evening the division entered the French capital. Upon their arrival the Germans found to their surprise that much of the city had been evacuated, with only some 700,000 of the 5 million of the city's inhabitants remaining. The rest had taken to the roads south of the city, trying frantically in vain to escape the German drive. The French government, however, had earlier moved from Paris to the city of Tours. It then moved again to Bordeaux. In this photograph German troops march triumphantly along the Avenue Foch in Paris following the French capital's capture. In the background is the Arch of Triumph (the Arc de Triomphe de l'Étoile).

SS troops in the Avenue Foch as a military band can just be seen passing round next to the Arc de Triomphe. A motorcycle combination can be seen moving along the side of the road. Note the soldier nearest to the camera: he is more than likely attached to the SS *Polizei* Division.

Following the capture of Paris, troops often went on sightseeing trips prior to their redeployment back to their home stations. In this photograph soldiers from *Das Reich* regiment *Germania* can be seen staring at the camera with the Eiffel Tower looming skyward behind them.

Leibstandarte troops prepare to cross a stretch of water during operations in Greece. The division attacked from Bulgaria through Yugoslavia and then on to Greece. It was in Greece against determined British and Commonwealth forces that the SS demonstrated their skill and tenacity and fought a number of fierce unrelenting but ultimately successful battles.

An SS 15cm field howitzer crew crosses over a bridge in their 8-ton Sd.Kfz.7 halftrack bound for the front line towing their ordnance. This particular gun was primarily designed to attack targets deeper in the enemy's rear. This included command posts, reserve units, assembly areas and logistics facilities. The 15cm gun was used as the standard German infantry heavy cannon and supported the German army into battle.

A 2cm FlaK 30 gun mounted on a halftrack during operations in the Balkans. This weapon could engage not only air targets but ground ones as well. With the vehicle's folding sides down the gun was very adaptable and could traverse 360 degrees, making it a very effective weapon of war.

SS troops more than likely part of the *Totenkopf* Division marching on a road in Germany prior to its deployment to the East in the early summer of 1941. The troops wear the standard infantryman's equipment and are armed with the 98k bolt-action rifle. Note the machine-gunner with his MG34 resting on his shoulder for ease of carriage.

Chapter Three

The Western Front
1944-45

On the eve of the Allied invasion of France, four of the ten German armoured divisions in France and Belgium were Waffen-SS. They consisted of the 1st SS.Panzer-Division *Leibstandarte Adolf Hitler*, 2nd SS.Panzer-Division *Das Reich*, 12th SS.Panzer-Division *Hitlerjugend* and the 17th SS.Panzergrenadier-Division *Götz von Berlichingen* named after a medieval hero fitted with an artificial iron hand. Even by this late period German intelligence could not confirm with any degree of accuracy where the main Allied invasion would take place. As a consequence the bulk of the Waffen-SS divisions were not located in the Normandy sector under the command of the 7th Army. The *Leibstandarte* was lying in the area of Bruges in Belgium where it had been resting since the spring of 1944 and had become part of the high command strategic reserve and was, therefore, under Hitler's direct control. *Das Reich* was still in the Toulouse area where the level of partisan operations had increased. The new *Hitlerjugend* Division had been transported by rail from Belgium and was moved close to its expected area of action between the lower Seine and Orne rivers, while the *Götz von Berlichingen* Division was stationed in Thouars in France.

The *Hitlerjugend* Division was the nearest of all the four Waffen-SS divisions to the actual Allied landing-point. On paper the division had over 20,000 soldiers deployed for action in Normandy. Although it was short of a number of armoured vehicles, the troops were well-equipped and armed. After nine months of intensive combat training their spirits were high and they were looking at the coming action with confidence. It was probably the best-trained and demonstrably effective unit in Normandy – on either side.

When the *Hitlerjugend* was eventually released to meet the Allied invasion on 6 June, the division was constantly strafed by fighters which disrupted the cohesion of many of the marching columns. By the following morning on 7 June, exhausted from more than a day's constant marching, the bulk of the *Hitlerjugend* had moved into the area north of Caen. By this time reports had confirmed that the enemy had managed to break through some parts of the coastal defences and push his attack inland.

Within hours, fighting against the Allied forces was finally unleashed. From their hideouts and freshly-dug trenches the youths crashed into action, opening up a ferocious barrage of fire on British and Canadian positions. Although the continuous attack from the air disrupted the grenadiers' assault, the teenagers of the 12th SS fought on. Many of the Allied soldiers were shocked at seeing teenagers in SS uniforms. It was their first encounter with the *Hitlerjugend* generation. For months prior to the invasion of Normandy the Allies had ridiculed the *Hitlerjugend* as the 'baby-division' but to the soldiers who fought against the 12th SS, this was far from being a division of badly-trained teenagers. It was an elite unit that instilled fear and, at the same time, fought a battle that inspired even its enemies.

Over the next few days as the battle of Normandy intensified, the *Hitlerjugend* came under even heavier attacks. Still this did not discourage the grenadiers from being driven from their bombed and blasted positions, for they had been given orders to hold the enemy at all costs and prevent them from penetrating their lines and breaking through to the ancient city of Caen.

During the evening of 9 June the Panzer-*Lehr*-Division moved into line alongside the 12th SS after driving miles to the front from Chartres. The following day the 21st Panzer Division also moved up and helped the other two divisions to form the principal shield around Caen, with motley other ad hoc units that had retreated from the coastal sector. Over the following days and weeks the *Hitlerjugend*, *Lehr* Division and the 21st Panzer carried on fighting stubbornly in and around the city of Caen which was slowly being reduced to rubble.

By the morning of 26 June, the British finally unleashed a large-scale attack on Caen code-named Operation Epsom. During the day's fighting at least fifty enemy tanks were knocked out by the Panzers and PaK guns alone. However, the Panzer-grenadiers took a heavy battering and in some areas a number of battalions were totally wiped out along with their commanders. Over the next few days the Allies continued to strike out, smashing into the 12th SS lines and causing massive damage to their positions. In the days leading up to July the British, endeavouring to expand their bridgehead, became increasingly incensed by the conduct of the *Hitlerjugend* Division, who fought so tenaciously when its cause was so clearly lost. This dogged determination had managed to finally blunt the Epsom operation, which conse-quently prevented it from acquiring the high plain south of Caen. In spite of this success the division was badly depleted and its survivors exhausted. Most of the German forces around the city were in desperate need of being replenished.

On 5 July, news reached Army Group B that Hitler contemplated having the *Hitlerjugend* relieved. However, three days later the SS divisions were once again fighting another battle for Caen, code-named by the Allies as Operation Goodwood. Once again these 'boys' were the core of the defence and fought out the battle in the ruins around Caen with an aura of being indestructible, even though their ranks had been greatly depleted after weeks of continued defence. As the battle reached its peak, Hitler ordered the city to be held at all costs. However, with no more reserves left and ammunition rapidly running out, the Hitler youth were withdrawn and instructed to take on a new defensive position in the rear.

By 11 July the *Hitlerjugend* was relieved by the *Leibstandarte Adolf Hitler* Division which took command of two units that remained in action. For nearly a week the *Leibstandarte* battled in the Caen region in a desperate attempt to stem the advancing Allies. During the battle SS grenadiers fought a desperate close-quarter action that saw both sides sustaining terrible casualties. Although Operation Goodwood would be soon called off, both the British and Canadians continued keeping seven of the remaining nine Panzer divisions occupied in the Caen sector.

Six divisions of the American First and Third armies had meanwhile moved south on the western side of the Cherbourg peninsula. The only German armoured divisions in their path were the 2nd SS.Panzer-Division *Das Reich* and the 17th SS.Panzer-grenadier-Division *Götz von Berlichingen*. *Das Reich* Division had journeyed from Toulouse in the south of France and had been seriously delayed reaching the Normandy sector by partisan activity and the constant aerial attacks. The convoys of the division had been unable to carry out daylight movement and had crawled northwards through the darkness. All the Panzer divisions that arrived in the Normandy sector were in such bad shape that they needed days to regroup before going into action. German wireless signals were continuously filled with Panzer commanders requesting fuel, transportation, new routings and other important matériel needed to sustain their drive. *Das Reich* Division was no exception. It arrived exhausted in the rear areas of the battlefront between 15 and 30 June, nearly three weeks behind schedule, and was not inserted into the Normandy campaign until 10 July, by which time it had already suffered heavy losses. Despite its severe mauling by Allied bombing, the division was far from beaten.

All over the Normandy sector the Waffen-SS divisions continued desperately to try to keep the Allies in check. The Normandy countryside had created conditions that favoured the SS grenadiers. Clusters of trees, tall hedges, ditches and lack of roads frustrated the Allied armoured units seeking to destroy enemy tanks in open areas. Aided by this terrain the SS were able to defend positions for longer than the Allies expected possible, and as a result incurred huge casualties. Frequently the Allies watched their irrepressible foe come under a furious crescendo of mortar and shellfire and still they held their ground to the grim death. However, the savage Allied air attacks and naval bombardments gradually began to grind down the German defences. Movement was almost impossible by daylight and any vehicles that travelled during the day were attacked and destroyed.

By the end of the first week of August both the *Heer* and Waffen-SS divisions were fighting for survival. Corps and divisions remained in action on paper but were becoming a collection of small battles, shrinking down to battalion size. A catastrophe now threatened the whole area as the Americans began to break out and the Normandy campaign became mobile. To save the German forces in Normandy from being completely encircled and destroyed, a series of rapid withdrawals was undertaken through the Falaise-Argentan gap. On 16 August German forces continued retreating and crossed the River Orne. The *Hitlerjugend* Division desperately fought to keep the gap open. The bulk of the German armour, however, that had become trapped inside the pocket at Falaise fought a desperate battle to escape the impending slaughter. By 21 August the terrible fighting in what became famously known as the Battle of the Falaise Pocket drew to a catastrophic conclusion. The Waffen-SS had been dealt a heavy blow.

The Normandy campaign had been very costly for the Waffen-SS, with many of its elite units being annihilated. The *Leibstandarte* had suffered almost total destruction. *Das Reich* had some 450 men and fifteen tanks remaining; the *Hohenstaufen* had 460 men and some twenty-five tanks that had survived the slaughter. The 10th SS.Panzer-Division *Frundsberg* lost all of its tanks and artillery, while the *Hitlerjugend* had only 300 men remaining and no artillery.

Following the complete German defeat in France, remnants of their forces withdrew for rest and refitting. The *Leibstandarte* was withdrawn to Aachen; *Das Reich* limped back to the Schnee Eifel area; the *Hitlerjugend* was pulled out and sent back east of Maas in Belgium; and *Götz von Berlichingen* was moved to Metz. The *Hohenstaufen* and *Frundsberg* divisions were withdrawn to lick their wounds in a quiet backwater in Holland. It was a town called Arnhem.

With the huge losses inflicted on the Waffen-SS, the campaign in the West had proved, as had the battles in the East, that they could only delay the enemy, not defeat them.

Within months of the Normandy campaign the Waffen-SS would once again be ready and refitted for action. However, it was not to be another delaying action. This time the SS troops were to go over to the attack in a bold and daring offensive through the Ardennes region. This was to be known as the Führer's last gamble in the West.

By the summer of 1944 the Waffen-SS along with its *Heer* counterpart had come close to being completely annihilated on the Western Front. However, within months it had miraculously undergone recovery. Many of the divisions that had been battered in Normandy and then smashed to pieces in the Falaise Pocket and in the subsequent retreat across France were now rebuilt. New divisions had been raised or others brought in for refitting in Germany or on the Eastern Front. On paper it seemed that there was still hope but in reality many German units still seriously lacked transport and the appropriate numbers of officers and non-commissioned officers. A great number of units had barely half their proper requirement of the major items of equipment.

However, in spite of the shortages, in September 1944 just two months following the Normandy campaign Hitler decided to launch a great winter counter-attack in the West. The attack he envisaged would be through the Ardennes – the scene of his great 1940 victory – to capture the town of Antwerp. Fog, night and snow would be on his side. With Antwerp in German hands, he predicted the British and Americans would have no port from which to escape and this time the enemy would not be allowed to escape.

Here in the Ardennes a substantial number of divisions was assigned to the area, including four crack Waffen-SS: 1st SS.*Leibstandarte Adolf Hitler*, 2nd SS.*Das Reich*, 9th SS.*Hohenstaufen* and 12th SS.*Hitlerjugend*. These SS divisions were larger than the regular *Heer* Panzer divisions and totalled a ground strength between 16,000 and 20,000 soldiers, with three-battalion Panzergrenadier regiments, a slightly larger artillery regiment that included a battalion of *Nebelwerfer* and a *Sturmgeschütz Abteilung* with twenty or thirty assault guns. The SS also had a higher allotment of motor vehicles. However, they were still below their assigned strength for officers and non-commissioned officers, mostly because of the terrible losses sustained in Normandy.

The equipment used by the SS armoured formations in the Ardennes was generally excellent, although by this late period of the war it was still in short supply. The forces committed to the battle zone contained a number of independent self-propelled anti-tank and heavy tank battalions and several assault gun brigades, which were battalion-size formations. There were four *Schwere Panzerjäger* battalions, nominally equipped with a mix of *Jagdpanthers*, *Panzerjäger* IVs, and *Sturmgeschütz*.IIIs. The *Schwere Panzer* battalions contained the famous Tiger heavy tanks. Three of these units were committed in the Ardennes and the 501.SS was attached to the *Leibstandarte*. The lead element of the 501.SS *Schwere Panzer Abteilung* was commanded by the veteran armoured ace SS *Obersturmbannführer* Joachim Peiper, commander of the 1st SS.Panzer-Regiment.

For the attack in the Ardennes, the Waffen-SS was assigned for action with the 6th Panzer-Army, which was to deliver the decisive blow. It was commanded by *Oberstgruppenführer* Josef Sepp Dietrich, who had fought brilliantly on the Eastern Front and commanded the I.SS.Panzer-Korps comprising the 1st and 12th SS.Panzer divisions in the Normandy campaign. The 6th Panzer-Army contained all the four SS.Panzer divisions and was given the task of tearing huge holes in the American lines between the Losheim Gap and Monschau.

To the south of the 6th Panzer Army's sector lay General Hasso von Manteuffel's 5th Panzer Army and General Erich Brandenberger's 7th Army, which was the southernmost of the three armies committed to the offensive. Altogether the five

Panzer and Panzergrenadier divisions and thirteen infantry-type divisions consisting of *Fallschirmjäger* and *Volksgrenadier* troops were to be unleashed through the Belgium and Luxembourg countryside. The code-name for this historic offensive was *Wacht am Rhein* (Watch on the Rhine), and it was unleashed during the early morning of 16 December 1944.

The attack was opened up by 2,000 light, medium and heavy guns, howitzers and *Nebelwerfer* which poured fire and destruction onto enemy positions. Shell after shell thundered into American strongpoints. In the north 6th Panzer Army inflicted the heaviest barrage of fire. At least 657 guns and howitzers of various calibre and 340 *Nebelwerfer* were directed on American positions between Hofen and the Losheim Gap. For almost an hour without interruption shells screamed over the heads of the waiting German infantry. Abruptly the bombardment ended, leaving a stunned silence for a few moments. Then beneath the pines and camouflage netting, thousands of German soldiers began their 'historic offensive'.

The *Volksgrenadiers*, many going into battle for the first time, were excited at thethought of fighting an offensive that their Führer had said would drive the invaders from their homeland and win them the greatest victory since Dunkirk. The *Volks-grenadiers* were closely followed by the tanks and elite Waffen-SS Panzer divisions. The spearhead of the 6th Panzer Army was to be formed by I.SS.Panzer-Korps which had been tasked with smashing through American lines between Hollerath and Krewinkel and driving through to the Liege-Huy sector with the *Hitlerjugend* on the right flank and the *Leibstandarte* on the left. The I.SS.Panzer-Korps was given a particularly powerful *Kampfgruppen*, which was led by *Obersturmbannführer* Joachim Peiper and his powerful Tiger tanks.

The attack by Peiper went well. By 19 December his Tigers had reached Stoumont, where a vicious two-hour battle raged with the Americans trying at all costs to hold the town. When the town could no longer be held the Americans quickly retreated but Peiper's tanks pursued them for a few miles out of the town before eight of their own tanks were brought to a flaming halt at an American roadblock.

In spite of the successful German advance through the Ardennes, the Allies were now beginning to recover from the initial surprise and resistance was stiffening day by day. By 22 December the Americans began stemming the German drive. Coupled with the lack of fuel and constant congestion on the narrow roads, many German units were brought to a standstill. The fuel shortages were so bad that on 23 December Peiper's *Kampfgruppe* destroyed their vehicles and his remaining 1,000 men set out on foot for the German lines. The remnants of the *Kampfgruppe* then linked up with the *Leibstandarte* just before dawn on Christmas Day.

Along the entire front German soldiers were becoming increasingly exhausted. Even the Waffen-SS had become worn down. For days and nights in the wet and cold, they had pushed westwards towards a promised victory. Originally nourished by their early success and the apparent lack of resistance, their forces began to wither as shortages of rations, lack of sleep and the constant shelling and bombing from aerial attacks drained their energy. With the SS armoured spearheads bedevilled by broken lines of communication and lack of fuel, the Ardennes offensive began to grind to a halt less than two weeks after it was unleashed.

In a drastic attempt to assist the failing drive to the River Meuse, additional troops were thrown in to launch a new offensive in Alsace where the Americans had drained their forces in order to send reinforcements north into the Ardennes. The code-name was *Nordwind* and it was launched in earnest on New Year's Day with eight divisions spearheaded by an SS Korps consisting of the 17th SS.Panzergrenadier-Division *Götz von Berlichingen* and the 36th *Volksgrenadier*-Division. At first the offensive went relatively well but heavy resistance soon forced the Germans back. The subsequent commitment of the 10th SS.Panzer-Division *Frundsberg* and the 6th SS.*Gebirgs*-Division *Nord* failed to alter the situation in the area.

In the Ardennes the *Leibstandarte*, *Hohenstaufen* and *Hitlerjugend* divisions were heavily embroiled in fierce fighting around the town of Bastogne. The German capture of the town was not a symbolic one. It was essential to the successful development of their offensive through Belgium. Around the smouldering town the Waffen-SS fought with great energy and determination. Both sides incurred huge losses but still the Americans were resolute in defending the town and preventing the enemy from gaining entry.

During the first days of January 1945 the weather became even more appalling, with temperatures falling to around zero. Fighting through fog, sleet and deep snow caused discouragement and pessimism to spread on both sides and even the crack SS divisions began to falter. Around Bastogne the Germans were eventually forced onto the defensive and driven back. Nearly 12,000 German troops were killed attempting to capture Bastogne and 900 Americans died defending it, with another 3,000 killed outside the perimeter. From the pulverizing effects of ground and aerial attacks, the Germans had left behind 450 tanks and armoured vehicles.

The defeat outside Bastogne was yet another major blow to the German command and marked the turning-point of the offensive. All across their battered front fighting had become harder and resistance was difficult to overcome. Troops constantly found themselves beating the enemy only at terrible cost, only to find a few miles further on that fresh, well-armed American forces were waiting for them.

With so many Allied troops being deployed in the Ardennes, Hitler was slowly forced to realize how dangerous the war in the West had become. On 8 January, with more than 100,000 Germans dead on the battlefield, the Führer grudgingly ordered the remnants of the forward units to fall back to a line running south from Dochamps in the Samrée-Baraque de Fraiture area to Longchamps, 5 miles north of

Bastogne. Even more significant were orders for the mighty elite SS Panzer divisions to go over to the defensive. The 6th SS.Panzer-Army was withdrawn into reserve under Hitler's personal command and he also called back remnants of his foremost fighting machine – the *Leibstandarte* – from the Bastogne area. Panzers coming off the assembly lines were diverted from the Ardennes back to the Eastern Front and there were no more propaganda broadcasts in Germany about the 'historic offensive'.

By 24 January all four Waffen-SS divisions that were initially committed to the Ardennes campaign were withdrawn and ordered to Hungary in a drastic attempt to throw the Red Army back across the Danube and to relieve the capital, Budapest. As for the remaining forces in the Ardennes sector they were withdrawn and the remaining units were back over the Rhine by 10 February, preparing to fight the last battle of the Reich.

By early February 1945 German forces in the West were slowly being driven back. Along the defensive front remaining German divisions with handfuls of anti-tank and artillery guns were strung out along the front lines and were almost totally un-protected. Along whole areas of the front the once-proud Panzer divisions had been reduced to skeletal formations on a stricken field. They were now not only vastly outnumbered but seriously lacking in fuel supplies, lubricants and ammunition. When parts of the front caved in, armoured formations were often forced to destroy their equipment so that nothing was left for the conquering enemy. The Germans no longer had the manpower, war plant or transportation to accomplish a proper build-up of forces.

Despite the enemy's overwhelming superiority, German forces prepared their defensive positions along the German frontier and dug in. Many soldiers, especially those fighting in the ranks of the Waffen-SS, decided that their fate would be met out on the battlefield. However, much of the German forces that were thrown together to defend the Reich and protect the route into Germany were manned by inexperienced training units. Some soldiers were so young that in their rations they had sweets instead of tobacco. All of them were ordered to stand and fight and not to abandon their positions. Terrified at the prospect of retreating, which would warrant almost certain execution, many reluctantly opted to bury themselves deep into a foxhole or bunker. Here they hoped the western Allies would give them a chance to surrender, instead of burning them alive with flame-throwers or blowing them to pieces by hand grenade.

Although many SS soldiers were aware that the war was at its end, many still retained intense unit pride which often assured they would do their duty to the bloody end. By April 1945 the SS divisions in the West were virtually non-existent. What names remained were shadows, their ranks partially filled with a motley col-lection of men from the *Heer*, Luftwaffe, *Volkssturm* and *Hitlerjugend*. However, unlike their SS counterparts, they were not fighting with fanaticism in the name of their beloved Führer; they were compelled to fight on the battlefield for survival.

Many of the SS saw their end on the battlefield, fighting for the last strongholds. Towns and villages often saw SS troops dug-in and defending their positions to the last round. Even in front of Berlin, the last bastion of defence in the Reich, these fanatical soldiers fought on with massive losses.

As fighting soldiers, it was never doubted in the eyes of the Anglo-American forces that the SS were an elite band of men who fought with skill, courage and effectiveness. However, in captivity it was clear that many were arrogant, fanatical and unrepentant regarding the terrible acts of cruelty and barbarism that they had committed both on and off the battlefield.

An SS soldier on a road somewhere in Italy. He is standing in front of a light Horch cross-country vehicle and is holding a tortoise. It was in August 1943 that Hitler ordered the transfer of his elite SS Panzer Corps from the Eastern Front to Italy following the Italian capitulation in July. This type of sudden shift became characteristic of the employment of the crack SS divisions during the second half of the war, as Hitler used them as a 'fire brigade' to reinforce trouble spots. Note the lettering on the rear of the vehicle 'Abstand 30m' (spacing 30 metres) to ensure that vehicles did not bunch together in convoy, and the white paint applied to enhance visibility for night time driving.

A portrait photograph showing a young SS soldier on the left and his friend who has joined the ranks of Rommel's Afrika Korps. By 1943 it became apparent that the southern theatre of operations both in North Africa and Italy was collapsing. Rommel had lost his grip in the desert in May 1943 and Italy had surrendered to the Allies later in September 1943. This undoubtedly put incredible stress on the German arsenal and vital men and equipment required to prop up the Eastern Front were now being hastily shifted to the south.

Moroccan prisoners being led away under the watchful eye of an SS soldier during heavy fighting in southern Italy. It was the 4th *Tabor* of Moroccan Goums that fought in the Sicilian campaign, landing at Licata on 14 July 1943 and attached to the US Seventh Army. It was in May 1944 that three Goumier *groupes*, under the name *Corps de Montagne*, were the vanguard of the French Expeditionary Corps attacked through the Aurunci Mountains during Operation Diadem. It was here that many losses were inflicted on the Allies. The Moroccans fought very well but in a number of places were cut off by German forces and captured. The Moroccans were probably the most effective troops in the Allied armies deployed in Italy, especially in mountainous terrain.

At an SS command post in Italy and a commanding officer hands a piece of paper to a motorcycle dispatch rider. Italy's mountain spine provided the Waffen-SS with many opportunities for a good defence. Throughout the Italian campaign the Germans took advantage of this natural asset by incorporating Panther tank turrets and huge concrete emplacements into their defensive lines, which stretched across the Italian landscape.

SS FlaK-gunners guard the water's edge against aerial attack. As the Allied air force started to inflict heavy casualties by 1944, the Luftwaffe, *Heer* and Waffen-SS divisions became well-equipped with 2cm FlaK 38 guns. This gun had a practical rate of fire of 120 rounds per minute with a maximum horizontal range of 4,800 metres, which was particularly effective against both ground and aerial targets. Thousands of these FlaK guns were used in the defence of Italy in a desperate attempt to delay the Allied onslaught. However, like so much of the German armour employed on all fronts, they were too few or too dispersed to make any significant impact on the main enemy operations which were already capturing or encircling many of the key towns and cities.

A photograph taken while a 8.8cm FlaK gun is being readied to fire its projectile against an enemy target.

The crew of a 7.5cm le.IG18 during a fire-fight as they engage the enemy with their gun. Although the gun was one of the first post-First World War weapons to be issued to the *Heer* and Waffen-SS, it remained in service on all fronts until the end of the war. A typical infantry regiment controlled three infantry battalions, an infantry gun company with six 7.5cm l.IG18 and two 15cm s.IG33 guns, and an anti-tank company initially equipped with twelve 3.7cm PaK 36 guns, but started to be replaced in first-line units with the 5cm PaK 38 in late 1940 and this in turn by the 7.5cm PaK 40 from November 1941.

A photograph taken during operations in Italy showing the Waffen-SS with their VW Type 166 *Schwimmwagen* (literally floating/swimming vehicle) amphibious four-wheel-drive off-roaders. These vehicles were used extensively in Italy where rivers and streams were a common obstacle.

Two commanders dressed in the summer camouflage smocks survey a map in their Volkswagen *Schwimmwagen*. This vehicle was an amphibious car used extensively by both the *Heer* and the Waffen-SS during the war. The nearest man is decorated with the *Ritterkreuz* (Knight's Cross).

An interesting photograph showing a column of 166 *Schwimmwagen* amphibious vehicles halted in an Italian town. The terrain in Italy for vehicle movement was often hindered by steep ravines, mountains and many rivers. These vehicles were very versatile and were used extensively during operations against military and countering the growing resistance groups.

A VW *Typ* 166 *Schwimmwagen* halted in a field during summer operations in Italy. By this period the Waffen-SS and their *Heer* and Luftwaffe counterparts were slowly being driven northward by strong and determined Allied forces.

A photograph showing a typical mortar crew in action. A mortar crew usually consisted of at least three members: the gunner controlling the deflection and elevation of the weapon; the assistant gunner loading the round at the command of the gunner; and the ammunition man preparing and handing over ammunition to the assistant gunner. The weapon illustrated was probably the best mortar of the war, captured from the Soviets and used by the Germans on the Eastern, Western and Southern Fronts the 12cm *Granatwerfer* 378(r), which was the German designation for these captured Soviet mortars. The weapon consisted of a circular base plate, the tube and the supporting bipod, weighing 628kg in action, with the base-plate alone weighing 282–284.93kg. Because of its excessive weight, a two-wheeled axle was utilized, enabling the mortar to be towed into action, the whole assembly weighing a hefty 559.89kg. The axle could then be quickly removed before firing. In German service the captured Soviet weapon and an improved German version (the *schwerer* 12cm *Granatwerfer* 42) fired the German-made *Wurfgranate* 42 round, filled with 3.1kg of high explosive.

A number of vehicles parked alongside a road somewhere in Italy. Note the divisional insignia of the SS *Leibstandarte* Division painted on the rear of the vehicle. When some of the elite divisions were transferred to Italy they played little part in the conventional war. Instead they were involved in the guerrilla campaign. The *Leibstandarte*, for instance, was given the task of guarding several vital road and rail junctions in the area of Trento-Verona. After several weeks the division was moved to the Parma-Reggio area. During this period the *Leibstandarte* was involved in several skirmishes with partisans, their actions leaving an indelible mark on the Italian population. The SS were very brutal and mass killings were quite common. Note the '*Abstand* 30m' lettering on the nearest vehicle and the white lines painted on the two nearest vehicles to aid visibility during night time driving.

An SS soldier belonging to the *Leibstandarte* sits on his Sd.Kfz.250 Alt light reconnaissance halftrack which is armed with the MG42 machine gun and protected by a splinter shield.

In a field and SS troops are taking cover before moving forward. Note the machine-gunner armed with the MG34 machine gun complete with fifty-round basket drum magazine.

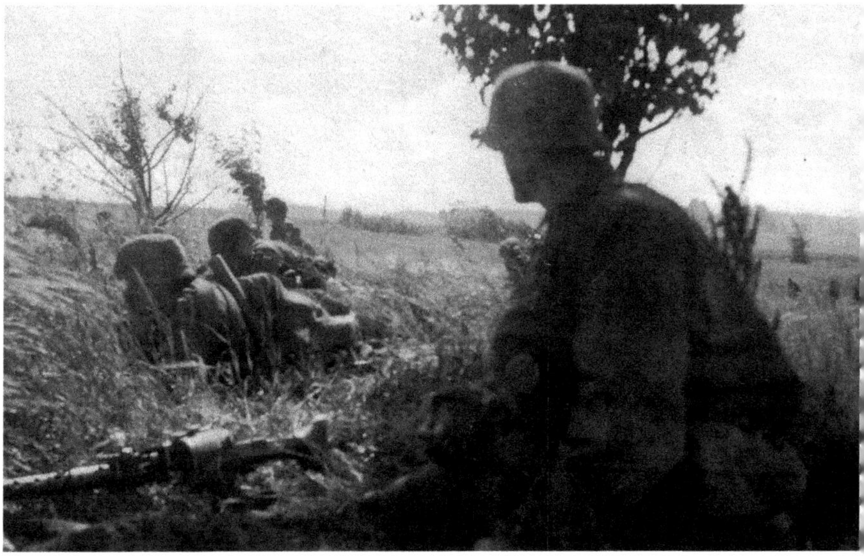

Coastal defence troops guarding the French coastline in 1944. A soldier armed with Kar98k bolt-action rifle and M24 stick grenade can be seen on duty. Many, but not all, coastal troops would be no match for the Allied invasion forces. Within hours of the attack many of the coastal forces would be dead or captured. It would be in the rear areas where elite SS divisions would be deployed to try to stabilize the threat from an inland Allied attack.

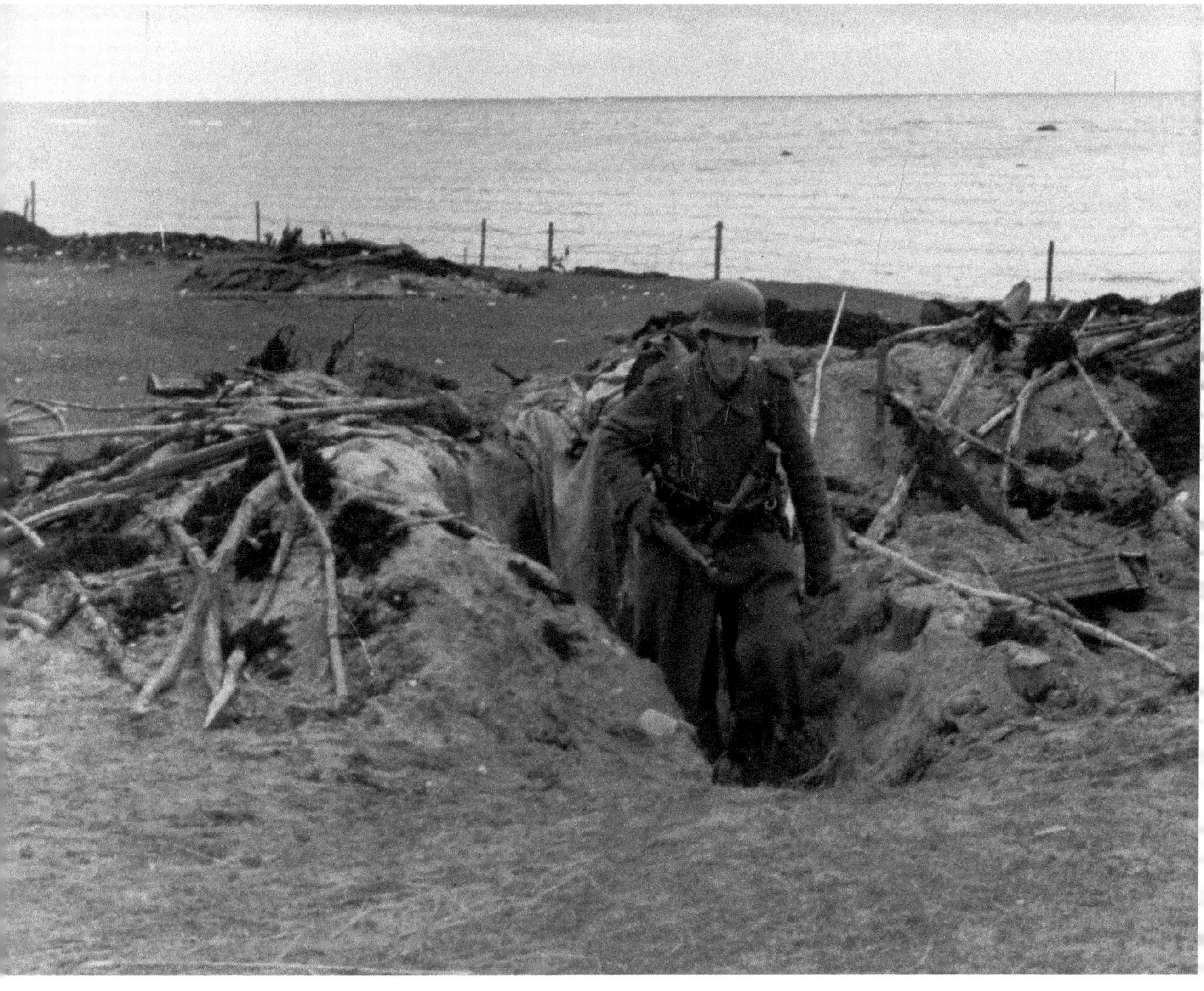

In June 1944 SS *Hitlerjugend* in a Normandy field armed with the 7.5cm le IG18 light infantry artillery piece. This particular weapon was used in direct infantry support. The gun was very versatile in combat and the crew often aggressively positioned it, which usually meant the piece was regularly exposed on the battlefield. The *Hitlerjugend* Division was the nearest of all the four Waffen-SS divisions to the actual Allied landing-point. On paper the division had over 20,000 soldiers deployed for action in Normandy. Although it was short of a number of armoured vehicles, the troops were well-equipped and armed. After nine months of intensive combat training their spirits were high and they were viewing the coming action with confidence.

SS troops move forward into action. From their hideouts and freshly-dug trenches the *Hitlerjugend* went into action against British and Canadian positions. Although the continuous attack from the air disrupted the grenadiers' assault, the 12th SS fought on.

A Tiger tank belonging to the 101st *schwere Panzer Abteilung* moving along a road in Normandy in late June or early July 1944. The unit markings were sometimes applied to the other side of the hull front. The vehicle is a mid-production specimen with rubber-tyred and interleaved road wheels. The division had been transferred to Normandy where it was part of the 1 SS Panzer-Korps which comprised the 101 SS Heavy Panzer Battalion, *Hitlerjugend*, 17th SS Panzergrenadier Division *Götz von Berlichingen* and the Panzer *Lehr* Division. Initially the *Leibstandarte* was deployed along the shores of the River Seine to counter any possible landing in the Pas de Calais. However, after the Allies had landed in Normandy the first units did not arrive in the Normandy sector until the night of 27–28 June. It took a further week until the entire division was regrouped for action, losing valuable time to counter the increasing Allied threat.

Two Panther tanks, probably belonging to the *Lehr* Division, parked in a Normandy village prior to their orders to the front. Note how much foliage has been attached to the tanks in order to try to break up their distinctive shape from the air. By this period of the war travelling by road during daylight hours was perilous for any tank crews. Consequently, much of the movement by road and rail was undertaken by the Germans at night to avoid high daylight movement losses.

A Panther tank somewhere in Normandy has been abandoned by its crew and blown up to deny its use to the enemy during a fire-fight in a village. Between June and July 1944 there were initially only two Panther-equipped Panzer regiments on the Western Front, with a total of 156 Panthers between them. From June through August 1944 an additional seven Panther regiments were sent into France, reaching their maximum strength of 432 in a status report dated 30 July 1944.

(*Above*) Two Panthers can be seen on the Western Front probably between June and August 1944. The towing cables suggest that the vehicle on the left has broken down or has become stuck, and is awaiting a tow from the other Panther Ausf.G. During the campaign in Normandy Panther crews found that although the Panther could deliver a lethal punch to the enemy, as a tank it was poorly suited to hedgerow terrain because of its width. The long gun barrel and width of the tank too often reduced manoeuvrability in village and forest fighting. As a direct result of this, many were knocked out of action.

(*Left*) An SS troop on motorcycles advances along a French road bound for the front. The smiles on the men's faces do not depict the seriousness of the situation. Many were told by their commanding officers that the Allies would bleed to death along the shores of France and there would be no immediate threat of them gaining any significant ground.

An SS soldier, probably a group leader, is about to jump off the Sd.Kfz.251 Ausf.D halftrack armed with his MP38/40 machine pistol. The halftrack is armed with an MG42 machine gun complete with splinter shield for local defence.

SS troops in a field during action against an enemy target. All over the Normandy sector the Waffen-SS divisions continued desperately to try to keep the Allies in check. The countryside here had created conditions that favoured the SS grenadiers. Clusters of trees, tall hedges, ditches and lack of roads frustrated the Allied armoured units seeking to destroy enemy tanks in open areas. Aided by this terrain the SS were able to defend positions longer than the Allies expected possible, and as a result the latter incurred huge casualties.

One of the most vital elements to sustain an army on the front lines was supply. Here in this photograph is a column of supply trucks destined for the front. However, with almost total Allied dominance from the air, movement was almost impossible by daylight and vehicles that travelled during the day were often attacked and destroyed. The tight vehicle spacing, which would be dangerous near the front, suggests that the photo was taken well to the rear and where strong AA defences were present.

A MG42 machine gun mounted on a sustained fire mount during operations in northern France in June or July 1944. Despite the adverse situation in which the German soldier was placed during the summer of 1944, he was still strong and determined to fight with courage and skill. However, by this period of the war both the *Heer* and Waffen-SS soldiers lacked sufficient reconnaissance and the necessary support of tanks and heavy weapons to ensure any long-term success.

A Panther commander surveys the terrain ahead through his binoculars, trying to establish the location of his enemy before proceeding forward into action. Note the foliage attached to the vehicle in order to help conceal it along the hedges and trees of Normandy.

SS troops move forward into action. Here the premier divisions did what they could in France to hold the Allies in check. The Waffen-SS fought alongside well-seasoned *Heer* and Luftwaffe divisions which gave them considerable support on the front lines. However, the German forces suffered huge casualties. Consequently, in order to make good these losses, many of the exhausted and depleted divisions had conscriptions of old men and low-grade troops. The method of recruitment generally produced very poor results. Not only was the number of recruits simply insufficient but the supply of good quality replacements into the German army was also beginning to show signs of strain and exhaustion. In the Panzerwaffe too many of the replacement crews did not have sufficient time for proper training and as a result losses soared. Lack of fuel and insufficient spare parts coupled with the lack of trained crews all played a major part in reducing the effectiveness of the German arsenal on the Western Front.

SS troops can be seen here making their way back to a MG42 machine-gun position with the weapon on a heavy mount for sustained fire. By the time the Allies launched their attack on the shores of northern France the German forces were ill-prepared for any type of large-scale offensive. The infantry's defensive positions required an efficient and regular supply of ammunition and the support of neighbouring units in order to hold their ground. Without this support the German forces were doomed. Commanders in the field were fully aware of the significant problems and difficulties imposed by committing badly-equipped soldiers to defend the depleted lines of defence. However, in the end, they had no other choice but to order their troops to fight with whatever they had at their disposal. The elite formations of the Waffen-SS had been removed from the Eastern Front in order to counter the threat in France. While many of the premier divisions fought well, delaying the Allied advance, they had in fact seriously weakened the forces available to hold the Russian Front and removed men and equipment that were desperately needed to prop up the disintegrating lines.

An SS soldier poses for the camera while sitting on the roof of a civilian vehicle that has been requisitioned for operational duties in the Waffen-SS. The photo shows a NSU-Fiat 1100 A (or perhaps the longer-wheelbase L model), an Italian design produced from 1939–1948, which was imported into pre-war Germany in limited numbers and then built under licence there. Note the blacked-out headlights and the SS licence plate.

A familiar sight by 1944, here troops can be seen with their 5cm PaK 38. Even by 1944 the PaK 38 was still widely used by the *Heer*.

An SS 8.8cm FlaK 36 gun complete with *Schützchild* (protective shield) in action against an enemy target. This FlaK gun was widely used as an anti-tank gun in which role it was formidable. On the battlefield it proved a very versatile weapon and continued being used in a dual role until the end of the war.

An SS trooper can be seen climbing up a tree to what appears to be an observation post set high up. Observation posts were key in determining the whereabouts and location of the enemy. Once located, the observer would relay the message via a field phone to the forward command post where the message would be forwarded to the commander in the field.

A well-concealed Sd.Kfz.250 Alt light halftrack during operations in northern France in the summer of 1944. During the day armoured vehicles were often halted and camouflaged until required to go into action. Movement was limited at all times.

SS troops advance through a field towards the battlefront. All across the front lines hundreds of defensive positions had been carefully selected, camouflaged and well-prepared for close-quarter combat. The Waffen-SS were determined at all costs to defend Normandy, even if it meant fighting to the death themselves.

Waffen-SS men climb out of what appears to be an old bomb crater.

Waffen-SS troops advance through undergrowth. The leading soldier appears to be holding an M24 stick grenade, while his comrade who probably is a troop leader is armed with an MP38/40 machine pistol.

A 7.5cm PaK 40 anti-tank crew belonging to the 12th SS Panzer Division *Hitlerjugend* during a fire-fight against an enemy target. By 1944, in addition to anti-tank weapons, a typical SS Panzer-Division was also authorized eighty towed and forty self-propelled 2cm guns and twelve heavy 8.8cm FlaK pieces. Less well-equipped grenadier and *Gebirgsjäger* divisions had eighteen towed and twelve self-propelled 2cm guns. These troops fought a desperate battle of attrition to hold on to their position around the town of Caen. However, following weeks of fighting and high losses in men and equipment the troops were forced from their positions and continued a defensive rearguard action, still fighting as they withdrew eastwards.

A Waffen-SS soldier surveys the area through a pair of binoculars in the Normandy sector. Along many parts of the front the Germans fought with fanatical resistance and held in a number of places. However, it came with a high price in men and materials. In spite of this the German soldier was still capable of meeting the highest standards, fighting courageously with self-sacrifice against considerable numerical superiority.

(*Facing page*) SS troops, probably at an observation post, are seen here with their Horch cross-country vehicle which has straw applied over it to help conceal it behind the stacked hay somewhere in the Normandy sector. Note the observer standing on the haystack with his 6 × 30 Sf.14Z scissor periscope observing the enemy. Forward observers were normally assigned to artillery batteries to establish observation posts among front-line infantry units. Their line of communication was often paramount in relaying important battlefield data.

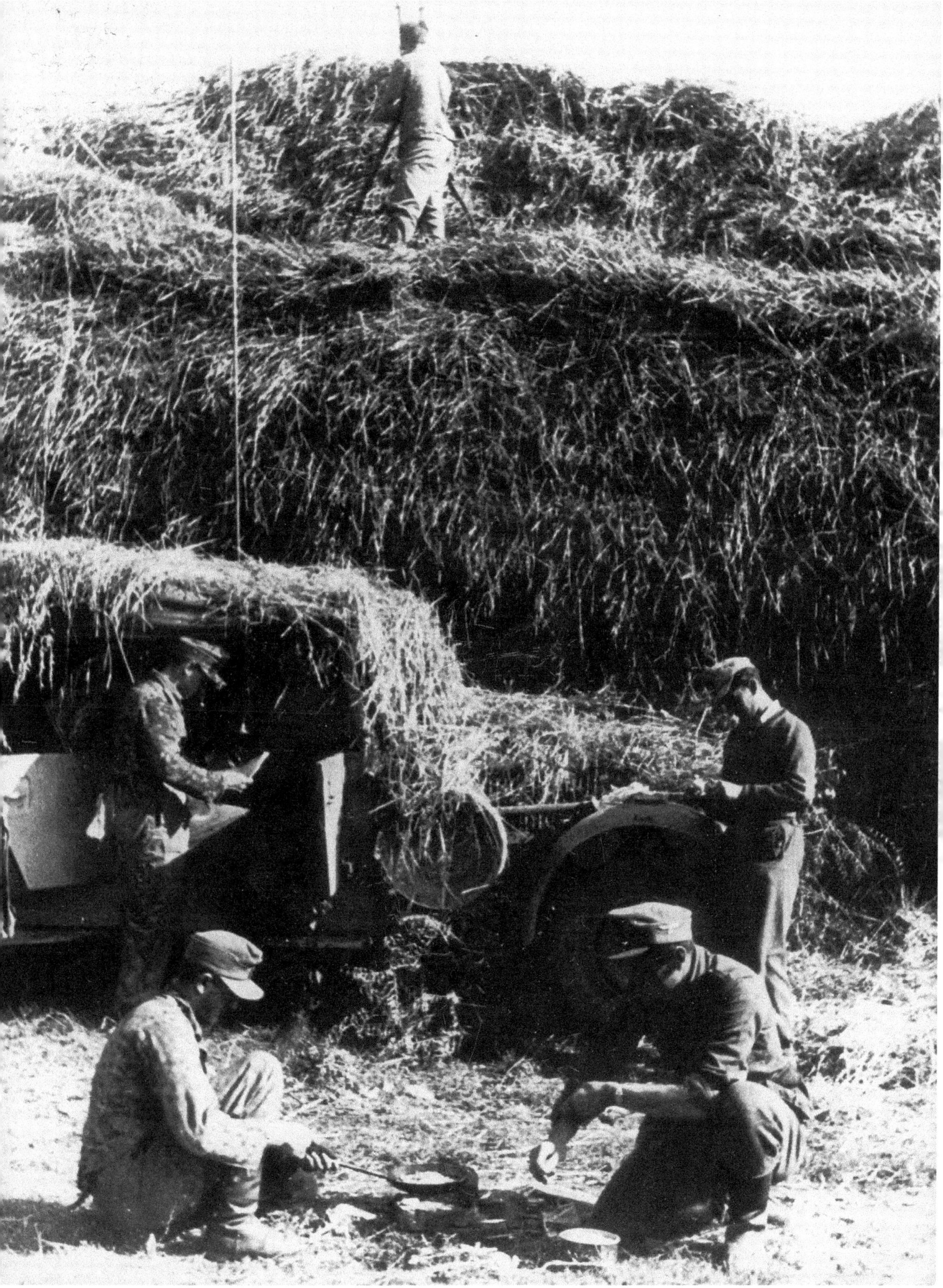

SS troops take cover from the incessant enemy aerial attacks that plagued the front lines in northern France.

A bicycle unit halted on a dirt track. Much of their kit has been attached to the bicycle. In the last year of the war the bicycle was one form of transportation that was utilized by both *Heer* and Waffen-SS troops due to the severe shortage of fuel.

Two photographs taken in sequence showing Waffen-SS troops in marshy ground. They are armed with the MP40 machine pistol. By this period of the war the MP38/40 sub-machine gun was manufactured in great numbers and issued to squad leaders, senior NCOs and front-line officers. It was regarded as one of the most effective sub-machine guns ever produced and used extensively within the ranks of both *Heer* and Waffen-SS regiments.

Two photographs showing the moment when 15cm *Nebelwerfer* 41s are fired in a defensive action against enemy positions. This deadly weapon fired 2.5kg shells from a six-tube mounted rocket-launcher. The projectiles could fire to a maximum range of 7,000 metres. When fired the projectiles screamed through the air causing the enemy to become unnerved by the noise. These fearsome weapons that caused extensive carnage to the enemy lines served in independent army rocket-launcher battalions and in regiments and brigades. The distinctive and long smoke trails helped the enemy pin-point the mortar positions for retaliation (assisted by special mortar detection radars) so that after firing it was essential to change the position of the *Nebelwerfer* batteries.

During operations in northern France, here SS troops are on the march. The almost total destruction of the Waffen-SS the campaign in the West had proved, as had the battles in the East, that the German forces could only delay the enemy rather than defeat him. Note the dismantled mortar equipment being carried.

SS troops preparing to leave a platform with supply trucks and other equipment on special railway flatbeds destined for the front. Foliage has been applied to all the vehicles and equipment in an attempt to break up the distinctive shapes and minimize the possibility of aerial attack while stationary.

Two SS soldiers pose for the camera as they prepare to board the train with the rest of their unit. A gun can be seen on the special flat car. Although travelling by train was regarded as perilous, especially during the last months of the war, it was still often the quickest method of moving men and equipment from one part of the battlefront to another.

Panther Ausf.G tanks have been chocked and ready for transportation to the front. Between 1944 and 1945 some 4,185 Panthers were produced. However, with such great demands put on these machines to fill the front lines on both the Western and Eastern Fronts, high losses were inevitable. Yet, in spite of the losses Panther crews continued to put up a formidable defence against the advancing enemy.

A column of Pz.Kfw.IV and StuG.IV assault guns halted on a road on the Western Front. From 1943 until the end of the war the assault guns were slowly absorbed into the Panzer units, Panzer and Panzergrenadier divisions of the *Heer* and Waffen-SS. Despite the StuG's proven tank-killing potential and its service on the battlefield both in offensive and defensive roles, the increased use of the StuG as an anti-tank weapon from 1942 onwards steadily deprived the infantry of the fire support for which the assault gun was originally intended.

A 2cm FlaK 38 gun mounted on the back of a Sd.Kfz.10/4 1-ton halftrack during summer operations in 1944. The sides of the vehicle are in the upright position. When the sides were down it allowed extra space on board the halftrack for the FlaK crew to manoeuvre easily. Note the Sd.Ah.51 trailer attached to the field containing ammunition. This weapon was usually served by eight men (four single 2cm FlaK guns would need a total of twenty-four men) on a single mount to give a combined cycle rate of fire of 1,800 rounds per minute. These lighter-calibre guns were much respected by Allied air-crews and were also devastating against light vehicles as well as soldiers caught out in the open. Such guns also armed a variety of vehicles on self-propelled mounts. Behind the Sd.Kfz.10/4 is a *Krupp Protze* 6 × 4 le gl LKw L2H43 1-ton light truck, and on the right is an Sd.Kfz.250 Alt light reconnaissance halftrack with what appears to be additional improvised side or roof protection on the upper hull sides.

One of the most important elements in maintaining vehicles on the front lines were the mobile maintenance units. Here in this photograph is one such unit that maintained many of the vehicles on the Western Front in 1944.

SS soldiers during a lull in the fighting can be seen next to an infantry support truck. By the summer of 1944 the Waffen-SS along with its *Heer* counterpart had come close to being completely annihilated on the Western Front. However, within months it had miraculously undergone recovery. Many of the divisions that had been battered in Normandy and then severely mauled in the Falaise Pocket and the subsequent retreat across France were now rebuilt.

A Waffen-SS FlaK crew during defensive operations on the Western Front during the early winter of 1945. This 2cm FlaK 30 gun had a practical rate of fire of 120 rounds per minute with a maximum horizontal range of 4,800 metres, which was particularly effective against both ground and aerial targets. A number of these mounted FlaK guns were used in the defence of the Rhine and Elbe in a desperate attempt to help delay the Allied onslaught. However, like so much of the German armour employed for defence, they were too few or dispersed to make any significant impact on the main enemy troops which were already capturing or encircling many of the key towns and cities.

A heavy machine-gun position. By late 1944 new German divisions had been raised or brought in for refitting in Germany or on the Eastern Front. On paper it seemed that there was still hope but in reality many German units still seriously lacked transport and the appropriate numbers of officers and non-commissioned officers. A great many units had barely half their proper allocation of the major items of equipment.

Waffen-SS troops pause during a lull in the fighting. In spite of the constant setbacks that plagued the front, the SS remained an irrepressible foe.

Two well-camouflaged SS soldiers armed with the lethal *Panzerschreck* (armour or tank terror), the popular name given by the troops to this weapon. The official name for it was the *Racketenpanzerbüchse*, or rocket tank rifle, abbreviated to RPzB. It was an 8.8.cm reusable anti-tank rocket-launcher developed during the latter half of the war. Another popular nickname was *Ofenrohr* or 'stove pipe'.

Waffen-SS troops can be seen inside a forest. Following the complete German defeat in France, remnants of the SS forces withdrew for rest and refitting. During their withdrawal many of the units spent time resting in the forests during the dangerous daylight hours when air attacks were likely and continuing their withdrawal at night.

As they withdraw across Western Europe SS troops take cover during a heavy exchange of fire.

A column of StuG.III Ausf.Gs making their way forward in the snow. On board is a mixture of *Heer* and Waffen-SS grenadiers clad in their winter whites. Panzergrenadiers were considered elite front-line units and were known for their performance at the front. Often they would advance into battle with assault guns and other armoured vehicles which offered them armour protection and mobility until they were close enough to attack enemy positions on foot.

SS troops wearing their winter whites and whitewashed steel helmets rest before continuing their march in the snow.

Waffen-SS troops in a forest pause in operations for some well-earned respite and warm food. An HF 12 small kitchen wagon can be seen next to other stationary vehicles. These mobile kitchens could also operate on the move, cooking stews, soups and coffee. The limber carried utensils and equipment. The troops nicknamed these kitchen wagons 'goulash cannons'. Many of the mobile kitchens were towed by animals but by 1944 were also seen pulled by an assorted range of vehicles.

Grenadiers hitch a lift on board a column of whitewashed StuG.III Ausf.Gs led by a StuH. The StuH has an application of Zimmerit anti-magnetic mine paste applied over the armour plating. By late 1944 the anti-tank battalion was more or less motorized and consisted of an anti-tank company equipped with *Jagdpanzer* IVs, *Hetzers* or StuGs which were organized into three platoons of four vehicles and an HQ section of two vehicles, a motorized anti-tank company of twelve 7.5cm PaK 40 guns and a motorized FlaK company equipped with twelve 2cm or 3.7cm FlaK guns.

Field Marshal Model conferring with his men in late 1944/early 1945. In August 1944 Model was made commander-in-chief of Army Group B and OB West. Many of the commanders in the field as well as the soldiers looked upon Model as the Führer's troubleshooter. He had been the commander who had first introduced in early 1944 the 'Shield and Sword' policy on the Eastern Front, which stated that retreats were forbidden unless they paved the way for a counterstroke later. Out on the battlefield Model was not only energetic, courageous and innovative but was friendly and popular with his enlisted men. Although these were critical days for the German forces on the Western Front, Model was still determined to try to improve the situation by opening up the pockets, pulling the troops out and withdrawing them in order to build new defensive lines. Out on the battlefield the condition of the troops varied considerably. While some parts of the front were manned by demoralized troops, others were heavily defended with a formidable force. It was these demoralized troops at the front that Model wanted to infuse the front-line commanders with courage and determination to hold and not give an inch to both them and the enemy.

A photograph taken next to a VW *Typ* 82 *Kübelwagen* (bucket or tub vehicle) showing American prisoners being led away during operations in the Ardennes in December 1944.

In the snow in late 1944 or early 1945: a 2cm SS FlaK 38 crew during defensive operations. During the war these formidable weapons were found in SS mechanized FlaK battalions. German divisions also had additional anti-aircraft platoons and companies in their Panzergrenadier, Panzer and artillery regiments. However, by 1945 they were badly depleted with low stocks of ammunition.

In support is a Wehrmacht Sd.Kfz.251 Ausf.D halftrack advancing through a town. These vehicles were used extensively during the latter half of the war by both the *Heer* and Waffen-SS to transport Panzergrenadiers to the forward edge of the battlefield. Despite being lightly-armoured, they could maintain a relatively modest speed and manoeuvre across country and keep up with the fast-moving spearheads.

With enemy aircraft now ruling the skies many German divisions had increased their anti-aircraft battalions with each of them containing two or even three heavy batteries. This photograph shows an 8.8cm FlaK 36 gun complete with *Schützchild*. In various sectors of the front some units barely had enough Panzers to oppose enemy armour and called upon FlaK battalions to halt the Allied attacks. During this later period many FlaK guns came to be assigned dual purposes, which involved adding an anti-tank role to their operational duties.

Grenadiers armed with the deadly *Panzerfaust* ('tank fist') march along a road under the protection of a *Jagdpanzer* IV. With the drastic need for new armoured fighting vehicles, more second-generation tank destroyers were built. One such vehicle that came off the production line in 1944 was the *Jagdpanzer* IV. This vehicle, built on the chassis of a Pz.Kpfw.IV weighed 28.5 tons. The vehicle was equal to any enemy tanks thanks to its potent 7.5cm gun. The *Jagdpanzer* saw extensive service during the last months of the war and with its reliability and well-sloped thick frontal armour it became a highly efficient fighting vehicle.

SS soldiers with their Volkswagen Type 166 *Schwimmwagen*. The Type 166 was the most numerous mass-produced amphibious car in history. Note the *Panzerfaust* anti-tank projectors inside the vehicle. This recoilless projector consisted of a small, disposable preloaded launch tube firing a high-explosive anti-tank warhead, operated by a single soldier. The *Panzerfaust* remained in service in various versions until the end of the war. The weapon had warnings written in large red letters on the upper rear end of the tube, warning the user of the back-blast. After firing the tube was discarded, making the *Panzerfaust* the first disposable anti-tank weapon.

A close-up view of two King Tiger tank men taken in Budapest in 1945. Note the Zimmerit anti-magnetic mine paste on the turret. For additional armoured protection track links have been attached to the side of the turret. The mounting of spare track links would reassure a superstitious crew that the protection had been enhanced, but tests showed that at certain strike angles this improvised armour actually weakened the protection by causing shot traps.

SS troops hitch a lift on board a Pz.Kpfw.IV Ausf.H or J. The Pz.Kpfw.IV became the most common Panzer in the Panzerwaffe and remained in production throughout the war. Originally designed as an infantry support tank, it soon proved to be so diverse and effective that it earned a unique offensive and defensive role on the battlefield.

A series of photographs taken of Waffen-SS troops inside a forest during defensive action on the Western Front. A typical strongpoint deployed along the front contained a series of MG34 and MG42 machine guns on light and heavy mountings, an anti-tank rifle company or battalion, a sapper platoon that was equipped with a host of various explosives, infantry guns, an anti-tank artillery company with a number of anti-tank guns, and occasionally a self-propelled gun. If and when available there might also be Pz.Kpfw.IVs, Tigers, Panther tanks and a number of StuG.III assault guns, all of which were scraped together. This front-line defensive belt became a killing zone where every possible anti-tank weapon and artillery piece would be used to ambush Allied tanks. While an enemy tank was subjected to a storm of fire within the kill zone, special engineer mobile detachments equipped with anti-personnel and anti-tank mines would quickly deploy and erect new obstacles, just in case other tanks managed to escape the zone. Despite the weakened lines of defence when the Allies attacked, they were met by very strong resistance in a number of areas. Note the extreme youth of some of the soldiers.

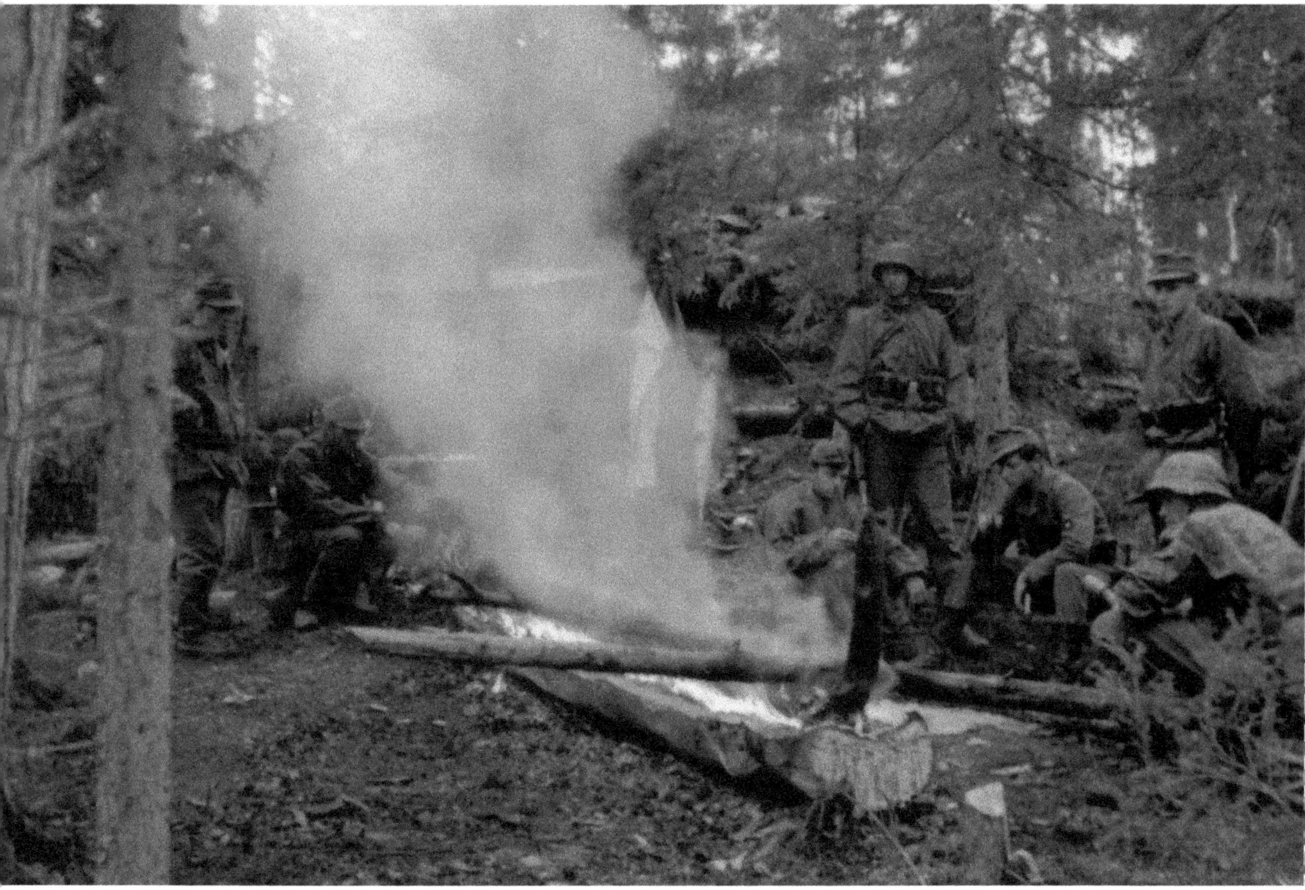

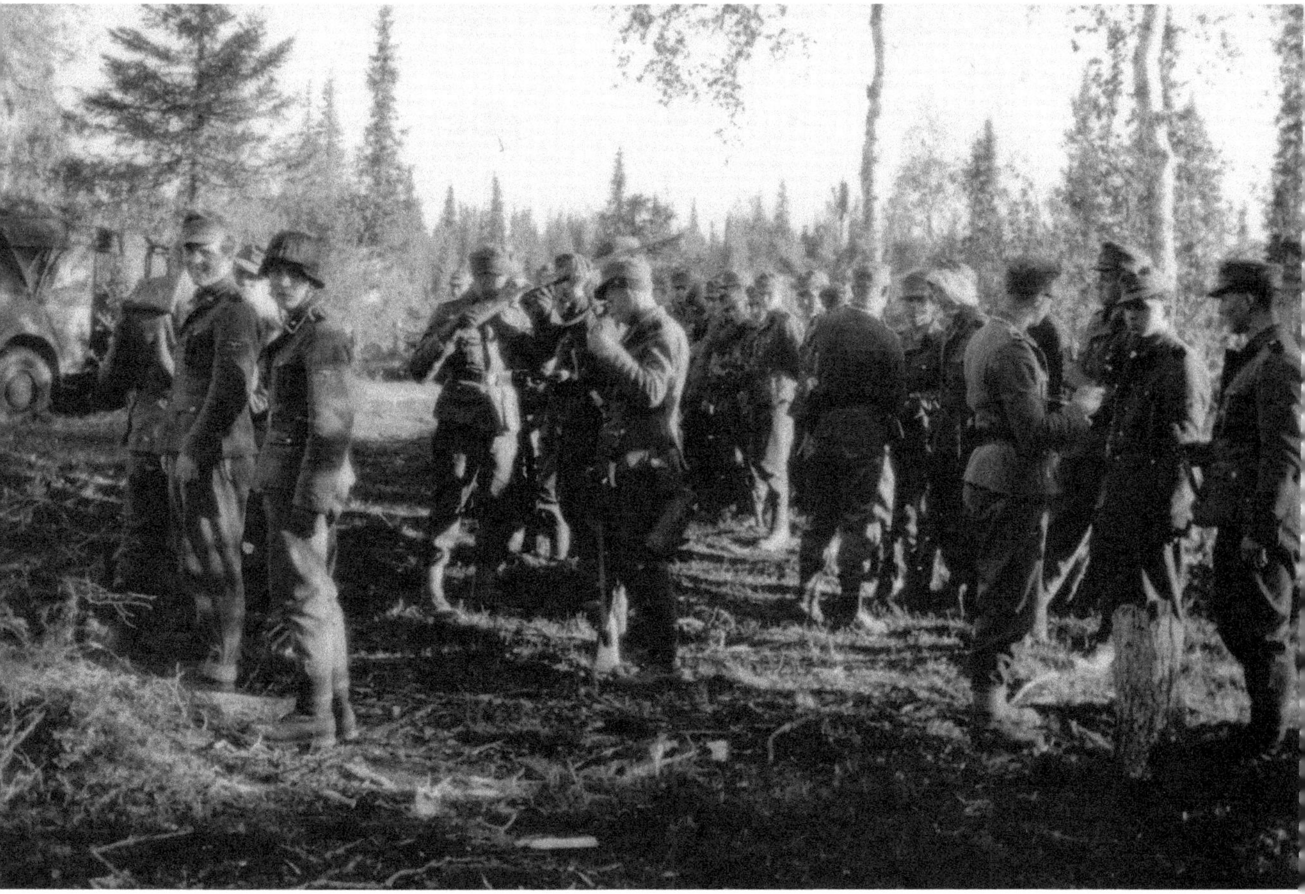

SS troops survey the terrain ahead. The bulk of the weapons and equipment used by the Waffen-SS throughout the war was more or less identical to that used by the *Heer*. A number of small arms, particularly those of foreign origin, saw considerable use in the units of the Waffen-SS due to the *Heer*'s initial reluctance to supply sufficient quantities of German-produced hardware to Himmler's elite force.

A Waffen-SS 8cm mortar crew preparing to fire one of the weapon's projectiles. Although the SS were slowly being driven further east by overwhelming enemy superiority, they were still fighting with fanatical determination on the battlefield.

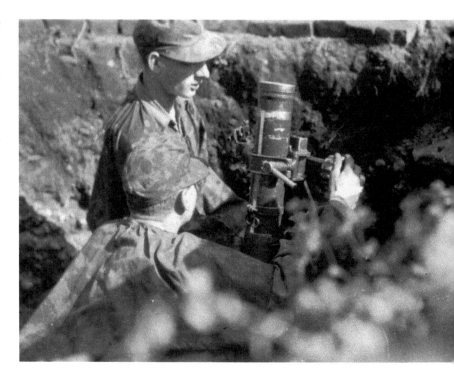

A photo taken at the moment a captured (possibly Czech, French or Soviet) heavy artillery piece is fired at an enemy target. Note the gunner plugging his ears. Late-production models such as this one had pressed steel wheels with solid rubber tyres and air brakes for motor towing. While these old howitzers were heavy and impractical for moving quickly to another position, they were used by both the Waffen-SS and *Heer* in offensive and defensive roles successfully until the end of the war.

A well-concealed SS grenadier inside his foxhole armed with the standard infantryman's bolt-action Kar 98k rifle and an M24 stick grenade.

A photograph showing an SS MG42 machine gun on a heavy sustained fire mount. In open terrain the MG42 heavy weapons squad would use their sustained fire mount to protect the flanks of the advancing rifle companies. However, in built-up areas the crews often had to operate forward with the rifle platoons and in light machine-gun roles with bipods only, but they were still sometimes able to take advantage of the situation and revert back to heavy machine-gun role.

SS troops tuck into their rations during a lull in the fighting. They appear to be sharing soup from one bowl. The troops were issued a march ration of sausage, cheese, dried bread, coffee and sugar in paper bags. However, during the last months of the war almost all rations had been exhausted and many troops had to rely on scavenging for what they could find, either from dead comrades, civilians or captured stocks.

SS troops pause in battle and have a cigarette before resuming operations. This photograph appears to have been taken in the last year of the war in the Balkans. Note the Waffen-SS soldier receiving a cigarette: he is armed with a Bergmann 9mm MP28 machine pistol. The Waffen-SS used a huge variety of weaponry, everything from small arms to heavy tanks. However, even these crack troops were curtailed by never-ending shortages and were supplied with various weapons and equipment in order to sustain them on the battlefield long enough to drive back the growing enemy forces. During the last two years of the war the Waffen-SS supplemented the finest hardware the German armaments industry could produce with whatever could be scraped together from German-made or captured stocks, in the same way that the *Heer* and the usually badly-equipped *Volkssturm* also had to make do as best they could.

A Tiger tank operating during the last weeks of the war. This tank served on both the Western and Eastern Fronts and with its potent firepower and thick armour it initially proved more than a match for any tanks fielded by the enemy. However, the introduction of more potent Allied tanks, especially the Soviet IS heavy tank series, ended its era of relative invincibility, which many crewmen often learned the hard way by remaining over-confidently aggressive. However, by this period of the war desperation had filled the ranks as the Tiger dwindled in numbers. As with other Panzer units, the once-vaunted Tigers continued to fight on until they were destroyed or they simply ran out of fuel.

Appendix I

Waffen-SS Weapons and Equipment

The bulk of the weapons and equipment used by the Waffen-SS throughout the war was more or less identical to that used by the *Heer*. A number of small arms, particularly those of foreign origin, saw considerable use in the units of the Waffen-SS due to the *Heer*'s reluctance to supply sufficient quantities of German-produced hardware to Himmler's elite force. The Waffen-SS used a huge variety of weaponry, everything from small arms to heavy tanks. However, even these elite troops were curtailed by never-ending shortages and were therefore supplied with various other weapons and equipment in order to sustain them on the battlefield long enough to drive back the growing enemy forces.

During the last two years of the war the Waffen-SS supplemented the finest equipment the German armaments industry could produce with whatever could be scraped together from German-made or captured stocks, in the same way that the Heer and the usually badly-equipped Volkssturm also had to make do as best they could.

Small arms

Pistole 08 pistol or Luger
Pisztoly 37M Hungarian service pistol
Frommer 7.65mm Hungarian pistol
Model 1914 Norwegian service pistol
Fallschirmjäger 42 automatic rifle
Maschinenkarabiner 42
Gewehr 41 (W) self-loading rifle
Maschinenpistole (MP) 28
Maschinenpistole (MP) 43
Sturmgewehr 44 assault rifle
Maschinenpistole (MP) 38
Maschinenpistole (MP) 40
Karabiner 98k bolt-action rifle

Infantry support weapons

Maschinengewehr (MG) 34
Maschinengewehr (MG) 42
5cm *Leichte Granatwerfer* (leGW) 36 mortar
15cm *Nebelwerfer* (NbW) 41 mortar
21cm *Nebelwerfer* (NbW) 42 mortar
Flammenwerfer (FmW) 41 flame-thrower
Stielhandgranate 39 magnetic anti-tank grenade

Anti-tank and anti-aircraft weapons

7.92mm *Panzerbüsche* (PzB) 38 anti-tank rifle
7.92mm *Panzerbüsche* (PzB) 39 anti-tank rifle
3.7cm PaK 35/36 anti-tank gun
5cm PaK 38 anti-tank gun
7.5cm PaK 40 heavy anti-tank gun
8.8cm PaK 43 heavy anti-tank gun
Faustpatrone 30 anti-tank rocket
Raketenpanzerbüsche (RPzB) 54 anti-tank rocket launcher
2cm *Flugabwehrkanone* (FlaK) 30
2cm *Flugabwehrkanone* (FlaK) 38
8.8cm *Flugabwehrkanone* (FlaK) 18 and FlaK 36 and FlaK 41

Artillery

10.5cm *Leichte Feldhaubitze* (leFH) 18 light field howitzer
7.5cm *Leichte Feldkanone* (leFK) 18
7.5cm *Feldkanone* (FK) 40
10cm *Kanone* (K) 18
15cm *Schwere Feldhaubitze* (sFH) 18 heavy field howitzer
21cm *Mörser* (Mrs) 18 heavy howitzer

Armoured cars and halftracks

Armoured cars

Sd.Kfz.221   Sd.Kfz.261
Sd.Kfz.222   Sd.Kfz.263
Sd.Kfz.223
Sd.Kfz.231
Sd.Kfz.234
Sd.Kfz.260

Artillery prime mover halftracks

Sd.Kfz.2

Sd.Kfz.6

Sd.Kfz.7

Sd.Kfz.8

Sd.Kfz.9

Sd.Kfz.10

Sd.Kfz.11

Light armoured reconnaissance halftracks

Sd.Kfz.250 series (12 variants)

Light ammunition carrier halftracks

Sd.Kfz.252

Sd.Kfz.253

Medium armoured personnel carrier halftracks

Sd.Kfz.251 (22 variants)

Panzers

Pz.Kpfw.III (later variants)

Pz.Kpfw.IV (later variants)

Pz.Kpfw.V Panther

Pz.Kpfw.VI. Tiger.I

Pz.Kpfw.VI. Tiger.II

Assault guns and tank destroyers

Sturmgeschütz (StuG.III) (later variants)

Sturmgeschütz (StuG.IV)

Panzerjäger Marder.I

Panzerjäger Marder.II

Panzerjäger Marder.III

Panzerjäger Nashorn

Jagdpanzer.IV

Jagdpanzer.IV/70 tank destroyer

Jagdpanzer.38 (t) *Hetzer*

Jagdpanzer.V Jagdpanther

Self-propelled artillery

Panzerjäger Hummel

Panzerjäger Wespe

Appendix II

Order of Battle:
Western Front 1940
(under OKW command)

OKH Reserve

German Second Army
  5th Infantry Division
German Ninth Army
I Corps
XVII Corps
XXXVI Corps
XXXVIII Corps
XXXIX Corps
XLII Corps
XLIII Corps

German Army Group A

Commanded by Colonel General **Gerd von Rundstedt**
(Chief of Staff – Lt.Gen. Georg von Sodenstern)

German Fourth Army – Colonel General **Günther von Kluge**
(Chief of Staff – Maj.Gen. Kurt Brennecke)
    II **Corps** – General of Infantry Carl-Heinrich von Stülpnagel
       12th Infantry Division – Maj.Gen. Walther von Seydlitz-Kurzbach
       31st Infantry Division – Lt.Gen. Rudolf Kämpfe
       32nd Infantry Division – Lt.Gen. Franz Böhme
    V **Corps** – General of Infantry Richard Ruoff
       62nd Infantry Division – Maj.Gen. Walter Keiner
       94th Infantry Division – General of Infantry Hellmuth Volkmann
       263rd Infantry Division – Maj.Gen. Franz Karl

VIII Corps – General of Artillery Walter Heitz
    8th Infantry Division – Lt.Gen. Rudolf Koch-Erpach
    28th Infantry Division – Maj.Gen. Johann Sinnhuber
XV Corps – General of Infantry Hermann Hoth
    5th Panzer Division – Lt.Gen. Joachim Lemelsen
    2nd Infantry Division (mot.) – Lt.Gen. Paul Bader
    7th Panzer Division – Maj.Gen. Erwin Rommel
Reserves
    87th Infantry Division – Maj.Gen. Bogislav von Studnitz
    211th Infantry Division – Maj.Gen. Kurt Renner
    267th Infantry Division – Lt.Gen. Ernst Fessman

German Twelfth Army – Colonel General **Wilhelm List**
(Chief of Staff – Lt.Gen. Eberhard von Mackensen)
    III Corps – General of Artillery Curt Haase
        3rd Infantry Division – Lt.Gen. Walter Lichel
        23rd Infantry Division – Lt.Gen. Walter von Brockdorff-Ahlefeldt
        52nd Infantry Division – Lt.Gen. Hans-Jürgen von Arnim
    VI Corps – General of the Engineers Otto-Wilhelm Förster
        15th Infantry Division – Lt.Gen. Ernst-Eberhard Hell
        205th Infantry Division – Lt.Gen. Ernst Richter
    XVIII Corps – General of Infantry Eugen Beyer/Lt.Gen. Hermann Ritter von Speck
        25th Infantry Division – Lt.Gen. Erich-Heinrich Clössner
        81st Infantry Division – Maj.Gen. Friedrich-Wilhelm von Löper
        290th Infantry Division – Lt.Gen. Max Dennerlein

German Sixteenth Army – General of Infantry **Ernst Busch**
(Chief of Staff – Maj.Gen. Walter Model)
    VII Corps – General of Infantry Eugen Ritter von Schobert
        16th Infantry Division – Maj.Gen. Heinrich Krampf
        24th Infantry Division – Maj.Gen. Justin von Obernitz
        36th Infantry Division – Lt.Gen. Georg Lindemann
        76th Infantry Division – Maj.Gen. Maximilian de Angelis
        299th Infantry Division – Maj.Gen. Willi Moser
    XIII Corps – Lt.Gen. Heinrich von Vietinghoff
        17th Infantry Division – Lt.Gen. Herbert Loch
        21st Infantry Division – Maj.Gen. Otto Sponheimer
        160th Infantry Division – Maj.Gen. Otto Schünemann
    XXIII Corps – Lt.Gen. Albrecht Schubert
        73rd Infantry Division – Lt.Gen. Bruno Bieler

    82nd Infantry Division – Maj.Gen. Josef Lehmann
    86th Infantry Division – Maj.Gen. Joachim Witthöft
  Reserves
    6th Infantry Division – Lt.Gen. Arnold von Biegeleben
    26th Infantry Division – Lt.Gen. Sigismund von Förster
    71st Infantry Division – Lt.Gen. Karl Weisenberger

Panzer Group 'Kleist' – General of Cavalry Paul Ludwig Ewald von Kleist
(Chief of Staff – Maj.Gen. Kurt Zeitzler)
  XIV Corps – General of Infantry Gustav Anton von Wietersheim
    9th Infantry Division – Lt.Gen. Georg von Apell
    13th Mot.Division – Maj.Gen. Friedrich-Wilhelm von Rothkirch
    9th Panzer Division – Maj.Gen. Alfred Hubicki
    10th Panzer Division – Lt.Gen. Ferdinand Schaal
    Infantry Regiment 'Grossdeutschland' – Lt.Col. Gerhard von Schwerin
  XXXXI Corps
    2nd Motorized Division – Josef Harpe
  Reserve
    27th Infantry Division – Lt.Gen Friedrich Bergmann

German Army Group B

Commanded by Colonel General **Fedor von Bock**
(Chief of Staff – Lt.Gen. Hans von Salmuth)

German Sixth Army – Colonel General **Walter von Reichenau**
(Chief of Staff – Maj.Gen. Friedrich Paulus)
  XVI Corps – General of Cavalry Erich Hoepner
    4th Infantry Division – Lt.Gen. Erich Hansen
    33rd Infantry Division – Maj.Gen. Rudolf Sintzenich
    3rd Panzer Division – Maj.Gen. Horst Stumpff
    4th Panzer Division – Maj.Gen. Ludwig Radlmeier
  IV Corps – General of Infantry Viktor von Schwedler
    15th Infantry Division – Maj.Gen. Ernst-Eberhard Hell
    205th Infantry Division – Lt.Gen. Ernst Richter
  XI Corps – Lt.Gen. Joachim von Kortzfleisch
    7th Infantry Division – Maj.Gen. Eccard von Gablenz
    211th Infantry Division – Maj.Gen. Kurt Renner
    253rd Infantry Division – Lt.Gen. Fritz Kühne
  IX Corps

XVI Corps
    3rd Panzer Division
    4th Panzer Division
XXVII Corps

German Eighteenth Army – Georg von Küchler
  Reserves
    208th Infantry Division
    225th Infantry Division
    526th Infantry Division
    SS *Verfügungstruppe* Division
    7th Airborne Division
    22nd Air Landing Infantry Division
    9th Panzer Division
    207th Infantry Division
  X Corps
    SS 'Adolf Hitler' Division
    227th Infantry Division
    1st Cavalry Division
  XXVI Corps
    SS *Der Führer* Division
    254th Infantry Division
    256th Infantry Division

German Army Group C

Commanded by Wilhelm Ritter von Leeb

German First Army – Erwin von Witzleben
  XII Corps
  XXIV Corps
  XXX Corps
  XXXVII Corps

German Seventh Army – Friedrich Dollmann
  Reserves
  XXV Corps
  XXXIII Corps

Appendix III

Waffen-SS Order of Battle: Ardennes December 1944

Units

277.*Volksgrenadier*-Division
I.SS-Panzergrenadier-Regiment.25
12.*Volksgrenadier*-Division
Grenadier-Regiment.48
Grenadier-Regiment.89
Fuselier-Regiment.27
3.*FlaK-Sturm*-Regiment
4.*FlaK-Sturm*-Regiment
340.*Volksgrenadier*-Division
3.*Fallschirmjäger*-Division (two companies from SS-*Pionier-Bataillon LSSAH*)

I.SS-Panzer Division

2.SS.Panzer-*Pionier-Abtleilung*.1
2.SS.Panzer-*Artillerie*-Regiment.1
12.SS-Panzer Division
Schwere-Panzerjäger-Abteilung.559
Schwere-Panzerjäger-Abteilung.560
SS.Panzer-Regiment.12
SS.Panzergrenadier-Regiment.25
SS.Panzer-*Aufklärungs-Abteilung*.2 *Das Reich*
9.SS.Panzergrenadier-Regiment.4 *Der Führer*

III.SS.Panzer-*Artillerie*-Regiment.2 *Das Reich*

SS.Panzergrenadier-Regiment
SS.*Werfer-Abteilung*.12
SS.*FlaK-Abteilung*
SS.*Aufklärungs-Abteilung*.12

SS-*Artillerie*-Regiment.12

SS.*Panzerjäger-Abteilung*.12
I.*Panzerjäger-Abteilung*.12
I.Panzergrenadier-Regiment.26

II.*Artillerie*-Regiment.12

Schwere Panzerjäger-Abteilung.560

II.SS-Panzer-Korps

2.SS.Panzer-Division
9.SS.Panzer-Division
10.SS.Panzer-Division
Schwere SS.Panzer-*Abteilung*.501
SS.*Werfer-Abteilung*
560.*Volksgrenadier*-Division
116.Panzer-Division
12.SS.Panzer-Divison
3.*Fallschirmjäger*-Division
277.*Volksgrenadier*-Division
3.Panzergrenadier-Division

Kampfgruppe Peiper

Main armoured vehicles used in the *Kampfgruppe* consisted of: Pz.Kpfw.IV Ausf.H or J, Pz.Kpfw.V Ausf.D (modified), A or G Panthers, Pz.Kpfw.VI Tigers, Pz.Kpfw.VI Ausf.B King Tigers, Bison Ausf.M Sd.Kfz.138/1, 150mm sIG 33/2 howitzer carrier (rear-mounted), and *Wirbelwinds*

SS-Panzer Regiment 1 LSSAH

I.SS.Panzer-Regiment.1

HQ Company

I.SS.Panzer-Regiment.1

Supply Company I.SS.Panzer-Regiment.1

1.SS.Panzer-Regiment.1
2.SS.Panzer-Regiment.1
6.SS.Panzer-Regiment.1
Schwere SS.Panzer-*Abteilung* 501

Supply Company sSS.Panzer-*Abteilung*.501

1.SS.Panzer-*Abteilung*.501
2.SS.Panzer-*Abteilung*.501
3.SS.Panzer-*Abteilung*.501

7.SS.Panzer-Regiment.1
9.SS.Panzer-Regiment.1
10.SS.Panzer-Regiment.1 (FlaK)

Maintenance Company, SS.Panzer-Regiment.1
III.SS.Panzergrenadier-Regiment 2
9.SS.Panzergrenadier-Regiment.2
10.SS.Panzergrenadier-Regiment.2
11.SS.Panzergrenadier-Regiment.2
12.SS.Panzergrenadier-Regiment.2
4.sSS Pz.Abt.501 (*Leichte*)

Supply Company, III.SS.Panzergrenadier-Regiment.2
13.SS.Panzergrenadier-Regiment.2
3.SS-*Panzerpionier-Bataillon*.1
FlaK-Abteilung.84
Fallschirmjäger-Regiment.9
I.Regiment.9
II.Regiment.9

Kampfgruppe Krag
(Commanded by SS-*Sturmbannführer* Ernst Krag)
SS.Panzer-*Aufklärungs-Abteilung*.2
2.SS.*Sturmgeschütz-Abteilung*
I.SS.*Panzerpionier-Bataillon*.2
I.SS-Panzer-*Artillerie*-Regiment.2
One medical support *Zug*

Appendix IV

Waffen-SS Divisions 1939–45

1st SS Panzer Division *Leibstandarte* SS Adolf Hitler

2nd SS Panzer Division *Das Reich* (previously SS *Verfügungstruppe* Division; later SS Panzergrenadier Division *Das Reich*)

3rd SS Panzer Division *Totenkopf* (previously SS Panzergrenadier Division *Totenkopf*)

4th SS *Polizei* Division

5th SS Panzer Division *Wiking* (previously SS Panzergrenadier Division *Wiking*)

6th SS Mountain Division *Nord*

7th SS Volunteer Mountain Division *Prinz Eugen*

8th SS Cavalry Division *Florian Geyer*

9th SS Panzer Division *Hohenstaufen*

10th SS Panzer Division *Frundsberg*

11th SS Volunteer Panzergrenadier Division *Nordland*

12th SS Panzer Division *Hitlerjugend*

13th Waffen Mountain Division of the SS *Handschar* (1st Croatian)

14th Waffen Grenadier Division of the SS (1st Ukrainian) (unofficially known as *Galizien*)

15th Waffen Grenadier Division of the SS (1st Latvian)

16th SS Panzergrenadier Division *Reichsführer-SS*

17th SS Panzergrenadier Division *Götz von Berlichingen*

18th SS Volunteer Panzergrenadier Division *Horst Wessel*

19th Waffen Grenadier Division of the SS (2nd Latvian)

20th Waffen Grenadier Division of the SS (1st Estonian)

21st Waffen Mountain Division of the SS *Skanderberg* (1st Albanian)

22nd SS Volunteer Cavalry Division *Maria Theresia*

23rd Waffen Mountain Division of the SS *Kama* (2nd Croatian)

23rd SS Volunteer Panzergrenadier Division *Nederland* (1st Dutch), formed after the dissolution of the 23rd *Kama* Division

24th Waffen Mountain Division of the SS *Karstjäger*

25th Waffen Grenadier Division of the SS *Hunyadi* (1st Hungarian)

26th Waffen Grenadier Division of the SS *Hungaria* (2nd Hungarian)

27th SS Volunteer Grenadier Division *Langemarck* (1st Flemish)

28th SS Volunteer Grenadier Division *Wallonien*

29th Waffen Grenadier Division of the SS (1st Russian)

29th Waffen Grenadier Division of the SS (1st Italian), formed after the disbanding of the 29th 1st Russian Division

30th Waffen Grenadier Division of the SS (2nd Russian)

30th Waffen Grenadier Division of the SS (1st Belarussian)

31st SS Volunteer Grenadier Division, variously reported as being named *Böhmen-Mähren* (Bohemia-Moravia) or *Batschka*

32nd SS Volunteer Grenadier Division *30 Januar*

33rd Waffen Cavalry Division of the SS (3rd Hungarian)

33rd Waffen Grenadier Division of the SS *Charlemagne* (1st French), given its number after the 3rd Hungarian Division was destroyed in battle

34th SS Volunteer Grenadier Division *Landstorm Nederland*

35th SS and Police Grenadier Division

36th Waffen Grenadier Division of the SS

37th SS Volunteer Cavalry Division *Lützow*

38th SS Grenadier Division *Nibelungen*